James Ritchie

An Australian Ramble

Or, a summer in Australia

James Ritchie

An Australian Ramble
Or, a summer in Australia

ISBN/EAN: 9783337312688

Printed in Europe, USA, Canada, Australia, Japan

Cover: Foto ©Andreas Hilbeck / pixelio.de

More available books at **www.hansebooks.com**

AN AUSTRALIAN RAMBLE

OR

A SUMMER IN AUSTRALIA

ORIENT LINE.
FORTNIGHTLY MAIL SERVICE
BETWEEN
England and Australia.

Steam-ships.	Steam-ships.
'AUSTRAL,' 5524 Reg., 7000 H. P.	'LUSITANIA,' 3877 Reg., 4000 H. P.
'CUZCO.' 3898 Reg., 4000 H. P.	'ORIENT,' 5365 Reg., 6000 H. P.
'CARONNE.' 3876 Reg., 4000 H. P.	'ORIZABA,' 6077 Reg., 7000 H. P.
'IBERIA,' 4661 Reg., 4200 H. P.	'ORMUZ,' 6031 Reg., 8500 H. P.
'LIGURIA,' 4548 Reg., 4200 H. P.	'OROYA,' 6057 Reg., 7000 H. P.

CALLING TO LAND AND EMBARK PASSENGERS AT

Gibraltar, Naples, Port Said, Ismailia, Suez, Colombo, Albany, Adelaide, Melbourne, and Sydney.

Steamers among the largest and fastest afloat, cuisine of the first order, electric lighting, hot and cold baths, good ventilation, and every comfort.

FARES FROM £17 17s. to £70.

Managers:—
F. GREEN & Co., 13, FENCHURCH AVENUE,
ANDERSON, ANDERSON & Co., 5, FENCHURCH AVENUE,
LONDON, E.C.
For Passage apply to the latter Firm.

AN

AUSTRALIAN RAMBLE

OR

A SUMMER IN AUSTRALIA

BY

J. EWING RITCHIE
(CHRISTOPHER CRAYON

LONDON
T. FISHER UNWIN
PATERNOSTER SQUARE
1890

TO

THE HONOURABLE EDMUND WEBB,

BATHURST, NEW SOUTH WALES,

THE FOLLOWING PAGES, MANY OF THEM WRITTEN

UNDER HIS HOSPITABLE ROOF, ARE

GRATEFULLY INSCRIBED

BY

THE AUTHOR.

CONTENTS.

CHAPTER I.

OFF TO AUSTRALIA.

PAGE

The *Orizaba*—Reasons for Travelling—The Bishop—Soda and Whisky—The Spanish Coast—Heroic Memories—Gibraltar—Wickedness of Naples—Port Said - 1—28

CHAPTER II.

EGYPT TO COLOMBO.

Coaling in Port Said—The Suez Canal—England the Main Support — Donkey-drivers — The Electric Light — Ismailia—Suez—Aden—The Red Sea - - 29—49

CHAPTER III.

COLOMBO TO ALBANY.

Prosperity of Colombo—Native Extortioners—Buddhist Temple—Life in the Streets—On the Indian Ocean—Stormy Seas guard Australia—English Coolness—Western Australia - - - - - 50—65

CHAPTER IV.

IN THE COLONY OF VICTORIA.

Melbourne Gleanings—Dr. Bevan—Night at a Bungalow—Cole's Book-shop—A Day at Sorrento—White Cruelty to the Aborigines—Coffee Palaces—Dr. Strong—The Presbyterian Church in Collins Street—The Late Peter Lalor—Ballarat—Romance of Gold Mining—Sydney and Melbourne compared—Australian Rogues—Suburban Melbourne—Victorian M.P.'s—Victorian Politics - - - - - 66—108

CHAPTER V.

A LITTLE ABOUT NEW SOUTH WALES.

Sunny Sydney—Public Buildings—Educational Establishments—Sanitary State—Its Climate—Bathurst—The Blue Mountains—Romish Aggression—Botany Bay—Old Days—A Wonderful Change—New South Wales Scenery - - - - - - 109—138

CHAPTER VI.

AMONGST THE BANANA BOYS.

Collision in Sydney Harbour—Brisbane—Queensland—The Banana Boys—Sir Samuel Griffith - - 139—146

CHAPTER VII.

SOUTH AUSTRALIA.

Holy Adelaide—Its Situation—Its Public Buildings—Its Mining-market—Dr. Arnold—Australian Plagues—Fleas and Mosquitoes and Serpents—Sunday Observance—The Macleay Mission—Number of Churches - - - - - - 147—165

CHAPTER VIII.

LIFE AT A STATION.

Mr. Dooleete's Station—Sheep-shearing—Patriarchal Life Improved—Snakes—Drought - - - 166—172

CHAPTER IX.

THE HEATHEN CHINEE.

His Persecution — His Usefulness — His Intellectual Ability - - - - - - 173—183

CHAPTER X.

THE LARRIKIN IN AUSTRALIA.

What the Larrikin is—A Social, Moral, and Political Danger—A Natural Foe of the Chinaman - 184—191

CHAPTER XI.

IN AN AUSTRALIAN VINEYARD.

Fruit Supply—Tintarra Wine—Mr. Thomas Hardy—The Temperance Question - - - 192—205

CHAPTER XII.

AN AUSTRALIAN MILLIONAIRE.

Mr. James Tyson - - - - - 206—211

CHAPTER XIII.

AUSTRALIAN FACTS AND FIGURES.

Increase of the Colonies—Further Emigration required—New South Wales and Free Trade—The Australian Type - - - - - - 212—223

CHAPTER XIV.

COMING HOME.

The Sea—Colombo—Arabi—Ceylon Tea—Stoppage in the Canal—Tilbury Docks—The Future of Australia —Australia as a Field for Emigration - - 224—235

AN AUSTRALIAN RAMBLE.

CHAPTER I.

OFF TO AUSTRALIA.

The *Orizaba*—Reasons for Travelling—The Bishop—Soda and Whisky—The Spanish Coast—Heroic Memories—Gibraltar—Wickedness of Naples—Port Said.

I SEND this from the *Orizaba*, one of the finest, if not the finest, of the fine steamers of the Orient Line that keep open the communication between this country and Australia; and this is how it came to pass. One day last summer I was standing on the deck of a steamer, when a gentleman remarked to me, 'I come from a country where they have had no rain for nine months.' 'Where is that?' said I. 'Australia,' was the reply; and immediately I made up my mind to go there. As is the custom of most of us, I talked the matter over with my friends, some of them in the first rank of the medical world. 'You can't do better,' was the unanimous reply; 'you will come back ten years younger,' said they all. Well, surely it is worth taking a little trouble and incurring a little expense, for a man—not to put too fine a point on it—presenting daily a more venerable appearance, to put back the clock, as it were, and to regain somewhat of his manly prime. 'What can I do for you?' said the family doctor to the mother of the Rothschilds, when he was summoned to her side; 'I cannot make you grow young again.' 'No,' was her ladyship's reply; 'I know you can't, doctor; but I wish to continue to grow old.' And here, just by taking a trip to Australia, and escaping the hardships of an English winter and spring, actually I shall achieve what the mother of the Rothschilds did not dare to hope for. Surely the attempt is worth an effort, especially when, owing to the kindness of a certain firm of publishers who shall be nameless, the question of expense was satisfactorily solved.

In these days of school-boards and universal travel a good deal has yet to be learned of our colonies. When I was younger, people in this country were in the most ludicrous state of ignorance as respects the size, area, wealth and value of what it is now the fashion to term the fifth quarter of the globe. At that time, say about 1830, there were not much more than 70,000 in all the land. Then Sydney Smith was writing of it as a region 'in which Nature has been so capricious, that she makes cherries with the stones on the outside, and a monstrous animal, as tall as a grenadier, with the head of a rabbit and a tail as big as a bedpost, hopping along at the rate of five hops to a mile.' Listen to Charles Lamb, as he writes, in his 'Essays of Elia,' to a friend in New South Wales: 'What must you be willing by this time to give for the sight of an honest man? You must have forgotten how *we* look. Do you grow your own hemp? What is your staple trade—exclusive of the national profession, I mean? Your locksmiths, I take it, are some of your great capitalists.' It was at that time the popular belief was embodied by Tom Hood as follows in 'A Letter from a Settler for Life in Van Diemen's Land,' wherein Susan Gale writes to her old friend and fellow-servant in Mount Street, Grosvenor Square: 'As soon as ever the Botes rode to Land I don't aggrivate the Truth to say their was half duzzen Bows apiece to Hand us out to shoar; and sum go so far as to say they was offered to through Speeking Trumpits afore they left the Shipside.' There is still a legend of a Missionary Society at home sending out a representative to Australia, and so carefully planning his route that he was to preach at Adelaide on the Sunday morning, and at Melbourne, some hundreds of miles away, in the afternoon, and that was before they had a railway. There are many who still think that a colony is a place where men are fortunate, as a late colonial governor remarked, if they enjoy three meals a day and a place to sleep in, where the inhabitants sit down to dinner in their shirt-sleeves, and think it a hardship if they take off their boots when they go to bed. But the greatest fallacy of all is the supposition that in a colony anyone can get a living, no matter how incompetent he may have proved himself at home. We laugh, but are we much wiser now? In Fleet Street last week, as I bade good-bye to a friend, he said to me, 'I have a boy who will be coming home just as you land. I sent him out with the best introductions. He has been six months in Melbourne and Sydney and elsewhere, and can find nothing to do, and now I have to get him home again.' It will be something if, in the course of my letters, and as the result of my inquiries, I shall be able to save fathers and mothers at home the trouble and expense and pain of such fruitless ventures, and it will be better still if I can help men and women at home to understand and realize what is being done by our fellow-subjects on the Australian Continent to plant that great land with Anglo-Saxon civilization and freedom and religion—if I can duly describe its cities and their people, their wealth and intelligence, their general activity and enterprise, their inner and public life. According to all accounts a good deal is yet to be told. Even Mr. Froude has omitted much that would interest the reader, and Dr. Dale has left something for the individual who may chance to follow in his steps. The fact is, the subject is too big for any one man.

I have said I send this from the *Orizaba*, one of the finest, if not the finest steamer of the Orient Line. Then there are the P. and O., who do not carry third-class passengers, and French and German steamers in abundance, to say nothing of other firms, who are always sending out steamers and sailing-vessels as well. As regards the latter, the firm of Devitt and Moore, of Fenchurch Street, deserve special mention, as they are the oldest people in the trade. Tourists who have the time to spare say there is nothing like a sailing-vessel for an Australian trip, and of the ships that sail in that direction, from all I hear, there are none that can equal the *Sobraon* (Captain Elmslie), and the *Macquarie*, in the Sydney trade (Captain Goddard, late of the *Paramatta*). All the fleet of this firm, however, bear a high character, and passengers, whether as regards accommodation or the commissariat, have no occasion to complain. The special objects of the managers of the Orient Company are to increase the facilities for the interchange of communication, and to promote the speed, safety, and, it may be added, pleasure of the passage. They are under contract with the Governments of New South Wales and South Australia to convey the mails fortnightly between England and Australia by way of Suez, and also run occasional steamers by the Cape of Good Hope. Since the Line was opened in 1877, upwards of 150,000 passengers have been carried to and fro, with all but total immunity from accident to life or limb. It cannot be doubted that the facilities thus afforded have added alike to the welfare and happiness of both the old world and the new. At home we are supplied with Australian produce, and Australia is a good customer in the English market. The service is performed by some eleven first-class steamers, varying from 3,000 to 7,000 tons. An old stager gave me the hint to choose one of the smaller vessels, on the plea that I should have better attendance on board. However, I prefer to follow the crowd, and have secured my berth on board the *Orizaba*, named after one of the highest mountains, somewhere, they tell me, in South America. Already she has carried the largest number of passengers ever taken by one vessel to Australia. She was built and engined by the Barrow Shipbuilding Company, the builders of the far-famed *City of Rome*. In the saloon there are chairs for 130 first-class passengers. The ship's company numbers 200. There are second-class and third-class passengers on board. Apparently there is little danger of starvation, as the provision-chambers of the ship are sufficient to supply fresh provisions for 1,000 persons from England to Australia. The promenade deck is grand; and as to the saloons and drawing-rooms, they are fitted up in palatial style, and the electric light by night makes the interior look like fairyland. I ought to be happy with all the provision made for comfort on board. But who can say what may happen when I am in the Bay of Biscay, or even after I have set foot on *terra firma?* Strange things are constantly occurring. The other day I heard of a good man in Essex, in one of its small towns, who, as duty required, went to his favourite chapel on the Sunday morning; on his return to his Sunday dinner he was rather astonished to find that in his temporary absence his wife and daughters had packed up and started to join the Mormons on the other side of the Atlantic. It is to be hoped that no such calamity may happen to me. As to myself, there is little danger of my doing anything rash, for 'he that hath wife and children hath given hostages to fortune,' as the great Lord Bacon told the world long ago.

It was not till Sunday morning that we left Plymouth, instead of Saturday. The fact was we had a tremendous addition in the shape of passengers and luggage to take on board, as all the people from the North come *viâ* Plymouth, besides the London passengers who are glad to escape the dangers of the Channel. On Sunday morning we had a short service in what is termed the drawing-room. The bishop, of course, was a colonial (you never go to sea without meeting one), and wore his official robes, though his reading-desk was but a small table, which was covered by the British flag. The bishop followed up the prayers with a five minutes' address, in which he said that a ship was like the world. In the world we were exposed to temptation, and so it was on board a ship. We were exposed to temptations from our fellow-passengers—an unkind reflection on some of us, I thought. Asking the purser what, from his wide experience of life on a ship, the peculiar form of temptation to which we were exposed was, his reply was 'whisky and soda'—a form of temptation of which, apparently, the bishop had nothing to say. The bishop does not interest me greatly, though he has kindly volunteered to read prayers every morning. The air of the bishop's lady is slightly subdued, as if the weight of her dignity were too much; *she* reads Church papers, whilst *he* evidently enjoys his novel.

But let me leave the bishop alone, and turn to things of a more worldly character. Poor Edgar Poe writes: 'There are four conditions of happiness in life, and one of them is life in the open air.' In this respect we are especially fortunate. We are no sooner out of the Devonshire mists than we are in the Bay of Biscay, calm as an infant on its mother's breast. We live in the open air. Passed Cape Finisterre after dark on Monday night, and steamed pleasantly down the Spanish coast, having an especially fine view of Cintra and the mouth of the Tagus. All along the coast were dotted, amongst the foliage, white villages, and towns, and villas, all basking in the summer sun. Heroic memories come to us as we pass over the seas where the *Captain* was lost, in consequence, it is to be feared, of defective seamanship, with her crew of picked men and some of our finest lads of noble birth. All along that coast, when Old

England was fighting for pre-eminence and power, and on those far-away hills has the noise of battle rolled, and not in vain, for the struggle that ended with Waterloo placed England in the first rank among the nations of the earth. From Tilbury's ancient fort to Gibraltar we are reminded how England, with her wooden walls and hardy sons, proudly swept the seas, and was a terror to the despots and a deliverer of the slave. Plymouth especially calls up a host of glorious names, as we think of Drake, and Hawkins, and Frobisher, and the Pilgrim Fathers. It was from Plymouth that Cook and Vancouver sailed, to give us New South Wales in the East and British Columbia in the West. As soon as we cross the Bay of Biscay we think of Corunna and Sir John Moore. Afar off are the heights of Torres Vedras, celebrated in the Peninsular War. Cape St. Vincent, a bluff 260 feet high, having a convent, on which is the lighthouse, reminds us of the brilliant victory won by Sir John Jervis, with Nelson and Collingwood fighting under his flag; and in a little while we are at Trafalgar, to which sailors still look as the greatest sea fight in the history of our land, and as the one which saved our national existence. And we step on shore at Gibraltar, which rises out of the water, with its endless rows of barracks and its few scattered villas, and make our way to the lightning-struck tower known as O'Hara's Folly—the O'Hara who was the friend of Johnson, and who ought to have married either Fanny Burney or Hannah More.

But it is idle to call up what to most of modern readers must be bare names, so soon, in this age of reading and writing and universal progress, do we forget the past. History in these mechanical days is getting as much out of fashion as theology. Let me write of living people; of men and women, poor creatures as they are at the best, to be brushed away as gossamer. There are just upon a thousand of us in the shape of passengers on board the *Orizaba*, and almost all are happy. The dark figure in the shape of Black Care we have left behind, as we have slipped out of English fog and cold into the region of cloudless nights and starry skies. We smoke, or read, or talk, or walk the deck, in a climate brighter even than that of an English summer in the leafy month of June. The ladies crochet or knit all day long in their lounging-chairs on deck, while the little ones play as if they had no fear or thought of the sea and its everlasting hunger for precious human life, and its cruel storms. What we should do with this unmanageable mass if anything were to go wrong no tongue can tell. All we can do is to hope for the best, for no

Parliament will ever go so far as to order that no ship should leave an English port without its sufficient complement of boats ; and if they did, no shipowner could carry on a profitable passenger trade. It ought not to be so, I know. What can one do? We are bound to travel, and we take the risk, whatever that may be, and trust to our sailors and captains, who are not half paid for the work they have to do. As it is, there is no life so pleasant as that of life on board one of our great passenger steamships. The *Orizaba* never rolls—well, only a little. The saloons are beautiful, the living is first-rate, the waiting is excellent, and the sleeping-berths are all that can be desired. By night, with the electric light all along the deck, the scene reminds you of the Arabian Nights, and mirth and music are everywhere ; I pity the poor people who have to spend their winter at home. It is now a real pleasure to live. The only thing one misses are the newspapers and the old familiar faces. Well, I am not sorry to be out of the way of the papers ; they only make me sick and sore as one reads the daily chronicle of poverty with which no one can grapple, and of crime which it seems impossible to repress, and the twaddle which envelops all. And as to the familiar faces, the further one travels the more one realizes all their loveliness and charm. For once the poet is right; absence does make the heart grow fonder.

'How do you like our little town?' said an Englishman to me as I was about to leave Gibraltar for our good ship, the *Orizaba*. 'Well,' said I, 'for a place to spend an hour in I like it amazingly.' 'Oh, that's about it!' was his reply. It seems to me, however, as I plough my way on the blue waters of the Mediterranean—not bluer, however, at present than what we have on the English coast—that a couple of days may be agreeably spent at the far-famed rock, of which, however, you get a very fair idea without stepping on shore. As your eye rests on the harbour you see it full of steamers, which seem to come and go at all hours. As I write a French steamer slowly glides by with the yellow flag denoting sickness of some kind on board. Before us is the town, on our left the old Moorish fort—the oldest building in the place—and on our right the hospital, with houses reaching almost to the end. All the space between is filled with yellow or white houses, save where a thick grove indicates the existence of the Alameda, a public garden, where the band plays, where the townsfolk promenade, and which, with its cactuses and geraniums in full bloom, looks bright and gay even in December. The company have so arranged that you can step into a boat and get rowed to shore and back for a shilling each way—an example which I recommend to the corporation of Gravesend.

I land, and declining a carriage drawn by mules amid the loud vociferations of the Spanish owners, turn to my left, and find myself in the main street, the only ugly building in which is the red-brick mansion in which the British Governor resides. All the houses are shops—full of the little trifles of Morocco manufacture, such as pipes and jewellery and gay mats and carpets, with which we are familiar at home. There are 20,000 Spanish residents, and the place swarms with them. There are some 5,000 British soldiers here, and they are *en evidence*, as was to be expected. They have five years to stop here at a time, and they evidently think that—as indeed it is—too long. One of the first things to interest you is the little graveyard on your right, in which the heroes of the siege were buried—shaded by trees, especially by a fig-tree of gigantic size and very old, as you can tell by the smallness of the leaf. A building which attracts your eye just before you enter the busy street is that of the Soldiers and Sailors' Institute, which is erected on a freehold site, and comprises on the ground floor a coffee and refreshment-bar, dining-room, bath-room, and lavatories; on the first floor a reading, writing, and recreation-room, with a small library; and above is a large hall for mission services, public meetings, Bible classes, and mothers' meetings. The soldiers and sailors, I fear, do not appreciate the advantages as they might, though Mr. Holmes, the superintendent, tells me at times the hall is more than filled. It is in the streets —or rather in the people that crowd them—the chief charm of Gibraltar lies.

The life of the place is *al fresco;* everyone seems out of doors. Carts drawn by mules or donkeys, with country produce, bright little carriages to hold two or four persons as the case may be, the English officer on horseback—all these block up the middle of the street; whilst on the narrow sideway you wind your difficult way amongst monks and nuns and dark-eyed Spanish women with the national head-dress, and Moors who shuffle along bare-legged, with slippers to their feet, their whole person enveloped in their ample, hooded brown or blue cloak, while some wear the picturesque turban, and others simply rejoice in the well-known fez. As I contemplate the motley group a black-eyed and black-bearded, aristocratic-looking Moor makes a dart at me with a couple of fowls; but, as I decline to purchase, he manages to ask me for a penny—and, let me add, in vain, for I could not think of insulting such a gentleman by offering him so ridiculously small a sum. But I see no beggars, and if the common people look dirty, at any rate they appear to be well fed. I fancy a good deal of British gold, somehow or other, finds its way into their pockets. There are no ragged scoundrels to be seen, such as infest our London streets and are the terror of suburban residents. As you pass, the shopkeeper stands at his door and bids you look at his miscellaneous wares.

Of British manufactures I see little, except the biscuits of Huntley and Palmer or Peek and Frean. I see no shops with books except the depôt of the British and Foreign Bible Society—but the people manage to live, nevertheless. Meat is but sixpence a pound. You buy beautiful oranges at a shilling a hundred. The only dear thing in the place is house-rent. Not a room is to be had under five shillings a week. Some of my fellow-passengers dined at the leading hotel, and they think, and I agree with them, that the charge was rather high. Only goats' milk is to be had, but as to cheap wine and low-priced spirits, they are to be procured in abundance, as two of our steerage passengers find out to their cost, as we leave them behind, and some who do manage to return may be termed rather fresh. The one great drawback of

Gibraltar, as regards the resident, is the absence of fresh butter. Alas! 'man never is, but always to be blest.' Of what avail are cheap cigars and wine and meat without fresh butter? Many have their bread buttered on both sides, and surely the humblest of us have a right to its being buttered on one, at any rate. But I may not linger, as I know the *Orizaba* will sail at the appointed hour; but we seem long in getting out of the crowd of boats, full of oranges and cigars, the proprietors of which are doing a roaring trade with the steerage passengers, who let down the money from the deck and receive in exchange oranges that will set them up for the rest of their journey, and away we go, leaving the Rock, at the bottom of which nestle the yellow rows of streets and houses, all with green or white lattices, whilst on its lofty head rests a drizzly cloud worthy of Devonshire itself. On the other side of us are the brown African mountains— we steer between them as the day closes in, and early in the morning I open my eyes to see afar on our left, the rocky outline of Spain, and then we lose sight of land, and can see nothing but the Mediterranean till early on Saturday morning we pass the first lighthouse on the coast of Sardinia. We are now coming to ancient history, but for that I refer the reader to Rollin, the terror of British youth in an age of which the present reader, intelligent though he may be in his way, has but a faint idea.

People who believe in Italian skies and summer seas ought not to trust themselves in the Mediterranean in December. We had what the captain calls 'a very heavy gale of wind,' after we left the 'Rock,' which lasted till we were almost in the Bay of Naples —a gale that sent all the ladies to bed, and damped the spirits of everyone on board. I had the full benefit of all the discomfort, as, instead of choosing a berth for myself, I left it to the officials, believing that in fine weather any berth is pleasant, and in bad weather all are equally disagreeable. But at any rate I should not have chosen the one allotted me, the very last of the berths forward (you are aware that in the boats going through the Red Sea the best berths are all forward, on account of the heat), but in my case, unfortunately, every wave that fell on the deck all night long came with a heavy thump overhead, which did not exactly secure me a good night's rest. However, all was forgotten as we steamed on Sunday morning past rocky Ischia into the famous Bay of Naples, which is far fairer than that of Swansea—in spite of all that gallant little Wales may say to the contrary. As I write the view is simply charming. All Naples is before me. On my left rises the lofty hill on which stands the Castle of St. Elmo. On my right are two high mountains—one of them, by the cloud of smoke hanging over it, and the flame of fire issuing from it, renders it quite unnecessary that I should ask anyone its name. You can tell Vesuvius at a glance. All the low land gradually rising away from the sea between them forms the site of delightful but dirty Naples.

I land as soon as the necessary formalities have been gone through—for they are very particular at Naples, and our purser and medical officer have first to go ashore in order to satisfy the authorities, a work sometimes extending over two hours. Fortunately, however, in a little while they are back, and we crowd on board the company's tender, which for half-a-crown conveys the passengers on shore and returns them safe and sound as late as eleven or twelve o'clock at night. Boats of all kinds are around us. One contains a bold swimmer, who performs all sorts of wonderful exploits ; others are laden with straw hats and baskets, and vendors of oranges and cheap jewellery and pipes, lava match-boxes, and amber mouthpieces. As I board the tender a pretty, smiling Italian flower-dealer puts a small camellia in my coat, which, however, I am ungallant enough to return. I fear she is like the flower-girls of Paris of whom

Tom Moore writes, that they spoil a romance with pecuniary views. In a few minutes I am on shore amid a crowd of dirty black-haired and black-eyed Italians, who offer me carriages and guides with an intensity of verbosity (recalling that of a certain Grand Old Man) sufficient to appal the stoutest heart.

I am rather disappointed at first. Cook's agents were to come on board, and one of them did put in an appearance, but that was all, which was a pity, as many of us were trusting to Cook as a tower of strength. In one respect I was especially disappointed. Cook was to take us all to Pompeii, give us lunch there, and bring us back for 12s.; but, alas! the King's uncle had died, and Pompeii was shut up, and so was the Museum. What a misfortune it is that royal personages should trouble us so much! While alive, of course we must do all we can for them; but surely, when dead, when they have fairly passed to where the wicked cease from troubling and the weary are at rest, it is hard that they annoy us still. Many of us may never again have a chance of seeing Pompeii. But I steer clear of the guides and start off for a three hours' prowl. What strikes the stranger is the loftiness of the houses, the narrowness of the streets, and the number of people. Locomotion in some is almost impossible, so dense is the crowd;

while it is the same in others in consequence of the number of equipages, chiefly open carriages drawn by black horses quite overdone with heavily-plated harness. To add to the difficulties there has been a slight shower of rain, and as the scavenger seems to be unknown, the streets are very slippery; I saw one little child run over in consequence. Another difficulty of the pedestrian is the number of stalls on each side, for the sale, apparently, of everything that can be brought into the street to tempt the purchaser.

Judging by the number of bookstalls, the Neapolitans must be very great readers, for I never saw so many anywhere else. In many of the streets that run between the leading thoroughfares, the passage is so narrow that it would be almost easy to shake hands across. All the lofty houses are yellow, with green latticed windows and balconies. In many of the churches into which I peeped Mass was in progress, and the attendance was large of men as well as women. In some of the streets the shops were handsome, though quite small, while in the great arches between were caves, as it were, where carriages and horses waited, apparently for hire, while in others the cave had been fitted up as a *café*. The further one got from the harbour, the finer were the shops and streets. In one I saw a statue of Petrarch, and in another of Dante. The place is like a rabbit warren, and just as populous. Priests and policemen were everywhere. Here and there was a religious painting on the side of a house, before which tapers were burning, and in one street I observed a crucifix, to which the passers-by took off their hats. I went into a *café* and watched some play at a billiard-table, much smaller and with much bigger balls than those in use among us. Omnibuses and tramcars abounded. Perpetual motion seemed to be the order of the day. Some of my friends patronized the English hotels, where the charges seemed to me dear. One thing, and one thing only, amused me; I stumbled on a kind of eating-house; on the outside was inscribed, *Déjeuner à la fourchette*, which was Englished underneath as follows: 'Breakfast to the fork.' I did not enter. I feared, as the English was so bad, that the cooking might be worse. Altogether, my impression is that Naples looks best at a distance and by moonlight, when a halo of soft light is thrown over bay and street and mountain far away, and the hoarse cry of its thousand street-sellers and cabmen and guides is unheard; when even the distant tinkling of the bells of its many churches no longer reaches the ear; when between you and the crowded city is a world of water calm and still.

At Naples we took up more passengers and more mountains of luggage. Our captain is in despair. That luggage question is the terror of his life. He says that there would be no need of it if the company would but establish a laundry on board; and why should they not? It would be a great convenience to everyone, and save a vast amount of trouble. The cabins are choked up with packages. It would be as pleasant again for the passengers if they could have their clothes washed on board.

I fear I did injustice to a dead royalty. I find, after all, it was simply the fault of the company's agent at Naples that most of us spent an idle day in that far-famed city. The distinguished representative of the distinguished Cook informed us that the Museum and Pompeii were closed that day, because the agent of the company with whom he came on board informed him such was the case. I find that they were not, and that a small party of our fellow-travellers visited both places; had lunch on shore, returned to the ship to dinner, and paid a visit to the theatre in the evening for a sum under £1 per head. As you may suppose, most of us were highly indignant at the conduct of the company's agent, and described him in terms that, with the fear of the libel law in view, it may be dangerous for me to report. I mention the fact that travellers may not be deceived by what they hear on board, but go on shore and act for themselves. Many of my fellow-travellers are Scotch. The Scotch, Mr. Charles Reade tells us, are icebergs with volcanoes underneath, and we had quite a volcano on board as we summed up the experiences of the unfortunate day. I own it served me right, for, as a rule, I only believe half that I hear. I ought to have started for Pompeii — by myself, trusting to luck to get into the place. I am glad, however, to be able to do justice to Cook and Sons, the friends of the traveller in every part of the world. It is seldom that they make a blunder, or their agents either.

In another respect I am not disappointed. 'The grand object of travelling,' wrote Dr. Johnson, 'is to see the shores of the Mediterranean. On those shores were the four great empires of the world—the Assyrian, the Persian, the Grecian, and the Roman. All our religion—almost all our laws—almost all our arts—almost all that sets us above savages has come to us from the shores of the Mediterranean.' To sail down the Mediterranean, past Capri—a sunburnt rock—past Stromboli, through the Straits of Messina, over the far-famed Scylla and Charybdis of the ancients, past Etna, though unfortunately hidden from our vulgar gaze by the clouds of night, is undoubtedly an immense treat. But the rest of the journey is rather monotonous, though we were favoured by fine weather, a fortunate circumstance, as this part of the Mediterranean is particularly liable to sudden storms; and if it were not for sea-quoits, and the still more popular game of dumps, which consists in throwing small flat balls with lead inside on to a white-painted square board, on which numerals from one to ten are inscribed, it would be rather hard work to get through the weary hours. At Naples an agent came on board with the London morning papers four days old, which sold readily at half a franc each, and the perusal of them has helped to kill an idle time, and, besides, afforded topics for general conversation. For pedestrian exercise the *Orizaba* is admirably adapted, as eleven times round the promenade deck is supposed to be a mile, and at certain hours every one is supposed to be doing his or her 'constitutional;' thus, what used to be considered one of the bad effects of life at sea, its confinement, is entirely got rid of. Captain Conlan, our commander-in-chief, when off duty, has a friendly word for us all; but I must say, if tobacco be a slow poison, some of us are in a bad way, for I think without exception all the male passengers smoke; and at Gibraltar, where tobacco and cigars are cheap, most of them replenished their exhausted stores.

The principal event after leaving the Straits of Messina is the appearance of Crete, by the side of which, with her snowy-capped mountains, we steamed for about five hours. From her rocky foreground, resting on the blue waves, rise three mountain ridges, the chief of which 'is many-founted Ida,' towering 8,000 feet above the sea. As a caution to travellers, let me assure them how much one of Smith's dictionaries would be appreciated. Smith, it may be, is correct, but he is pedantic. Lemprière would, perhaps, be better; in the home of legendary lore it is not wise to be over-critical. The Orient Company publishes a guide-book, but it is of little practical use, though it contains an immense amount of information, some excellent maps, and is a marvel of cheapness. You rarely get in such books what you really want to know. We have a professor on board, but professors nowadays are somewhat common. Men who shave and cut corns—men who examine your head, who risk their necks in parachutes, who excel in gymnastics, are called, or call themselves, professors; and I, perhaps because I know no better—probably it is so—may be a little sceptical as to the class. I always think of Barry Cornwall's lines in which he speaks of

> Professors of hall and college,
> With a great deal of learning and little knowledge.

And, alas! I have known many such. It amuses me more to talk to some of the third-class passengers. 'Ah, sir,' said one of them to me, as we steamed out of Naples Bay—'ah, sir, that is a very wicked city; it allus reminds me of Nineveh.' I was compelled to admit that I did not know much of the wickedness of either; but that I did happen to know that, excluding Jack the Ripper, there were not a few wicked people left in London. I always like to look at home before I begin censuring other people. There is a good deal of truth in the remark of the old Californian, when Sir Charles Dilke told him 'Californians in the Empire City were called the scum of the earth.' 'Them New Yorkers,' was the old man's reply, 'is a sight too fond of looking after other people's morals.'

Just as we are nearing the lowlands of Africa, and Port Said—a wretched place, where we stop a few hours to coal—is in sight, a death occurs on board; a tiny babe, weary of the world of which it knows so little, refuses to live any longer. In the drawing-room few of us know of the event, and the gaiety goes on much as usual. I rush on to the deck, and see a dark cloud of passengers at one end, and there is the Bishop standing at a red kind of box or reading-desk, repeating that grand burial service which is nowhere more impressive than when heard in the ocean's solitude, with nothing but the wide, wide sea below, and the clear, moonlight sky above. The parents are, of course, there to mourn, and the bearing of the little crowd is sympathetic. The poor little corpse, covered by the British flag, is placed on an inclined board, which is tipped over when the sentence 'we commit this body to the deep' is reached, and the sea receives its dead. I had only asked the doctor that morning what was the state of health on board the ship, and his reply was that it was as well as could be. Perhaps steerage passengers don't count, especially when babies. At any rate, the funeral is over, and we are taking our evening tea as if nothing of consequence had occurred—as if no tender mother's heart had been torn with anguish as she saw her babe fall a victim to the Reaper whose name is Death. Not for a moment did the ship slacken her career, and we press on to Port Said with all our might.

CHAPTER II.

EGYPT TO COLOMBO.

Coaling in Port Said—The Suez Canal—England the Main Support—Donkey-drivers—The Electric Light—Ismailia—Suez—Aden—The Red Sea.

UNDER a vermilion sky, as the sun sinks down into the west, we approach the land of Egypt—a barren land, kindly to neither man nor beast, fruitful only in sand, and hospitable only to the camel, who seems here to be a friend in need, patiently following his turbaned leader over the pathless desert. We have a little sand near Southport, we have more still on the Lincolnshire coast at Skegness, we have most of all on the Dutch coast, from Flushing to Scheveningen, that gay resort of the Dutchmen and the Germans; but they fail to give you an idea of the dreary and boundless waste of sand through which that wonderful old man, M. de Lesseps, cut his grand canal, which ought to have been done by Englishmen, and which perhaps would have been, had not Lord Palmerston declared in season and out of season that it could not be done, and that if it were done it could never pay. When we stopped at Port Said, looking as if only artificially raised out of the sea, I landed: partly to say I had planted the sole of my foot in Egypt—the land of the Pharaohs, of Joseph and his brothers, of Antony and Cleopatra, of Origen and Hypatia and early Christian hermits, of grand philosophies and theologies, which stir the pulses even of to-day—and partly that I might have an evening stroll in a place not at one time the safest for a white man to land, but which now is quite as free from danger as any London neighbourhood—the happy hunting-ground of the burglar and the thief. The fact was that at Port Said we had to coal; and as we landed after dinner, it was a new sensation to be rowed ashore by turbaned sailors, who were clothed in what seemed to me in the twilight very much like petticoats. It was rather risky, as the boat was crammed down to the water's edge. Nor was I much reassured as, after running up against the ropes and being nearly capsized, the man at the prow called out in broken English, 'Never mind,' to which I was obliged to reply that I did mind, and that I ventured to hope he would take care of our precious carcases. Apparently the advice was not thrown away, for after a few minutes' row, and after an attempt had been made to collect the fare, which we all firmly resisted till on *terra firma*, we landed where a couple of old women apparently, in reality sailors, were standing with lanterns ready to receive us. As the fare was only sixpence each way, I can't say that the Egyptian watermen were quite so exorbitant as some I wot of nearer home. There was not much to see at Port Said; but it was better to be there than on board ship while the process of coaling was going on. While at dinner there was a sound all round as if a million of monkeys were screaming and jabbering underneath. They were the coalheavers, on board the big barges laden with coal that surrounded us on all sides directly we had come to anchor. Each barge had two lights of burning coals, by the glare of which we could see the porters in strings of fifty at a time climbing up a ladder that led to the ship's inside, with coal-sacks on their shoulders, and streaming back again, all the while screaming, as seems to be the manner of the Arab tribe all the world over. They all scream. They screamed at us as we stood on the deck; they screamed at us as they rowed us ashore; they screamed at us as we walked the streets—or, rather, the one long street which forms the town till it is lost in the sand of the surrounding waste. On one side lies the market, and a mile or two beyond is the old Arabian town. Men of all nationalities are well represented in Port Said; but the Greeks have the best shops, where a fine trade is done in cigarettes, photographs, and richly-worked napkins, and helmets to keep off the sun in the Red Sea, and the other products to be met with in Turkish bazaars. In the street it was difficult to tell the men from the women, so weird and unearthly seemed their make-up in the evening gloom. Two of the dark bundles approaching me were, I concluded, women, as the faces were concealed —all but the dark, round eyes, from the dangerous glances of which, happily, my age protected me. The great attraction of the place was a large *café chantant*, which, however, I fancy, did duty as a gambling-house as well. On the bank, just as you land, is a large building calling itself the Hotel Continental; but as it was shut up, apparently it has not been a commercial success. The houses, or, rather, the shops —for there were nothing but shops to be seen—were all of wood and painted. On my return to the ship, which was covered with coal-dust, I found we had an Egyptian conjurer, who went through a performance such as we see any day in England. But I must not say a word against a gentleman who was so kind as to intimate that I was 'a big masher.'

Egypt to Colombo.

For a real Lotus-land, where it is always afternoon, commend me to the Suez Canal. It is a busy spot. No spot is busier. Steamers, especially English ones, are always passing up and down. It is an expensive spot. You are fortunate if your steamer has not to pay a thousand or two for the trip. The *Orizaba* has to pay £1,700 for going through; but that does not concern you, if you have taken your passage to Ismailia or Colombo, or one or other of the great Australian ports. All that you have to do is to sit still and enjoy yourself. There the good sailor and the bad one are equal. There you fear no north or south simoom, no seas mountains high (I have never yet seen them, and begin to believe in them only as I do in stories of mermaids and mermen, or in legends of the sea-serpent ever turning up at unexpected times and in unexpected quarters), no rough blasts of the winter winds, no equinoctial gales. The captain comes down from his bridge, the officers take it easy, and you really need not to drive dull care away. On that calm water, under that bright sky, you have no thought of time. All around you is still life—the boundless sands, the distant hills, the camels, and the Arabs encamped far away. All is repose, in the heavens above, as well as in the earth beneath. It is true the beggars here and there on the banks are a nuisance, but where are they not, either in the Old World or the New? For eighteen or twenty hours you are at peace—to read the last novel, to flirt with the last fancy of the hour; to dream, if you like, in the broad daylight of other days and other times. The big ship moves, but so slowly that you can scarce tell that you are moving at all. The stewards bring your meals as usual; your sleep is undisturbed. There is your morning bath, your accustomed cigar, your game of chess, or your rubber of whist. Ah, you are much to be envied! The pity of it is that the trip is so soon over; that the dream is soon dispelled; that the curtain so soon falls on the scene; that you have to get back again to the cares, and troubles, and struggles of real life.

In the matter of the Suez Canal, Englishmen are paying rather dearly for their faith in Lord Palmerston. It is to the credit of M. de Lesseps that he conceived the idea, got together the money, and carried it out, and by that means, as a patriotic Frenchman, secured for France an influence in Egypt which, not to put too fine a point on it, has not worked for the advantage of either Egypt or ourselves. The officials of the Canal are French, the official language is French, the neat little stations, with their painted wooden houses, protected here and there by a palm tree struggling for life, are pre-eminently French. Fortunately, Lord Beaconsfield bought some shares for the nation, which gives us a *locus standi*. But the Canal, you feel, ought to have been designed by British engineers and paid for by British gold. It is emphatically England that keeps it going. The stream of steamers ever sailing up and down by day or by night are chiefly English steamers built in British shipyards, sailed by British captains and officers, and filled with British goods. It is true France subsidizes her steamers to struggle with England in all parts of the world. It is equally true that Germany does the same, but they cannot beat the British merchant and shipowner, who will not yield without a fierce struggle the supremacy it has taken them centuries to build up and sustain, and if the Canal manages to pay a dividend, it is because of the constant passage of British ships. As we were steaming along the Canal in one of the finest steamers of the Orient line, and of any line, we met a French steamer on her homeward trip. Mounseer looked politely at our crowded deck—his own seemed deserted, though they do tell me that the accommodation on board the French ships is remarkably good, and then our steerage commenced singing with heart and soul 'Rule, Britannia.' They ought not to have done it, I know. It was a breach of good manners ; but if anywhere we may be pardoned for singing 'Rule, Britannia,' it is in the Suez Canal.

On leaving Port Said, in a few minutes you are in the Canal, which has been here protected from the shifting sand by a breakwater a mile and a half long. On Lake Menzaleh, to the westward, are to be seen wonderful flights and flocks of birds, including pelicans and flamingoes, to detect which, however, requires an uncommonly strong glass. Ships are piloted on the block system, under the control of the head official at Port Said, who telegraphs the movements of each ship as it slowly makes its way. At each of the stations, or 'gares,' there are signal-posts, and a ball above a flag says 'Go into the siding,' while a flag above a ball says 'Go into the Canal.' You see a good deal of the country, an utter, miserable desert at first, but soon hidden by the sand-banks. As you get nearer to Suez, wandering Arabs and droves of camels may be seen making their way along the burning waste, under the burning sun. All day and all night the heavens are wonderful. Now and then you meet a ship, and there is not much room to spare; now and then one is run aground, and it is often weary waiting, as it is inexpedient to go on shore and take a donkey-ride, in compliance with the request of the donkey-drivers, who seem to scent a stoppage from afar, and come to the bank, clamouring vociferously all the while. As you proceed you find the boys and girls on each side keeping you company, in hopes of the copper the kind-hearted visitor may feel inclined to throw them. It is needless to add that they are loosely clad, and are brown and sunburnt to look at. By night the electric light on the sandy bank has a singularly strange effect, which is more particularly apparent as another ship approaches, making the sand where it catches the light seem as if there were drifts of snow all round. As you enter the lakes the waters widen, and the speed is greater; the scenery is also a little more attractive. Away on your right is the land of Goshen, and Ismailia clusters prettily around the summer palace of the Khedive. Here you drop the passengers for Cairo, who are increasing in number every year—that part of Egypt becoming increasingly a winter resort, essential to the comfort and well-being of those who do not care for English cold and fog and rain. It is a wonderful change and a great relief for the asthmatic to spend a winter in Egypt. It is a pity that more cannot do so, but, alas! few of us can spare the time, and many of us have not the cash, and so a man must live where his bread is buttered, though to do so prolongs his pains at the same time that it shortens his life. As you look at Ismailia it seems a charming spot; however, the condition of the place is by no means sanitary, and danger lurks there under those green trees, beside those still waters. It has, however, been the scene of high life, as when the Canal was opened in 1869, when the Empress Eugénie, the Crown Prince of Prussia and the Empress of Austria took part in the ceremony. At a later date there was also exciting work in Ismailia when it became the basis of 'our only general's' brilliant campaign. The Canal and lakes were filled with transports and men-of-war, and to the town an army of 20,000 men looked for supplies. It was from thence they marched to fight the battle of Tel-el-Kebir, and to send poor Arabia prisoner for life to Ceylon, where, perhaps, after all, he is better off than he would have been had he stopped at home. His life would have been sacrificed had he remained.

Little of life is to be seen anywhere, but a few men are engaged in cutting away the sand, while camels bear it far away. They are ugly beasts, and never seem happy. They are, however, docile, and kneel down while the men fill the panniers with sand, when they rise up and walk away; or we come to a ferry where they are waiting to cross, and display the same patient, forbearing, half-starved look. The Egyptian donkey seems to me a far livelier animal. Now and then a dog displays itself on the bank, but he is rarely a favourable specimen of his race. Small steamers and barges, occupied in connection with the improvement of the canal, are also met, but the crew take little note of the white man, who, however, after all, has got such a hold on the land that it is questionable, whatever statesmen say at Westminster, whether it can ever be removed. It seems as if Egypt could never be let alone. True, it was a great country once, but that was long ago.

Again, we leave the Timseh, or the Crocodile Lake, behind, and make our way to the Bitter Lakes, through many miles of Canal. The lakes, history tells us, are the remains of a dried-up arm of the sea, where once flourished the ancient port of Arsinoe. Here we meet the slight tides of the Red Sea—that awful sea, whose waters at some seasons range to a temperature of a hundred. It was hot as we entered Port Said, it is hotter as we leave the Canal at Suez —the new port of which, with its modernized hotel, its rows of trees, and its modern warehouses, looks pretty from the water. Old Suez, a mile and a half from the new town, is visible long before we reach the fort. It is almost a pity that the steamers do not stay here a day or two. The old town is the most characteristic of old Egypt, and the rail will run you up there in a few minutes. It was the centre of the highway between Asia and Africa. All around is the desert, while mountains famed in history for ages are to be seen from afar. Egyptians tell me that Suez is preferable to Cairo as a health resort. One gentleman whom I met with told me that he wintered there every year. As we picked him up on my return, I was obliged to tell him that he did not look so well as when he went ashore a few months previously. In excuse he owned that he had suffered from a severe attack of rheumatic fever. It may be that Suez had nothing to do with that. Perhaps at Cairo they would have told me Suez was not a good place to go to. The water, however, is good, as we took a good many tons of it on board. It was well that we did so. At Aden, our next stopping-place, we found there had been no rain for nearly three years.

We stop a few hours at Suez, and early in the morning commence steaming down the Gulf of Suez, ere we float proudly over the waters of the Red Sea. At length it seems to me that we realize all that the poets have sung and painters have drawn of the Bay of Naples—unclouded skies and a sea of brilliant blue. All day long we are in sight of a romantic coast crowned with towering mountains, with diversified peaks that in the sun seem to glow with light and heat. As we approach they are brown or white or red, and then, behind, they seem dark and stern as they rise out of the sleeping waters. On our left are the Arabian mountains—Mount Sinai among them—more or less connected with the religion dear to all men of Anglo-Saxon race and tongue; the religion that has made modern history what it is—the religion which they tell us in the pulpit is yet to reign supreme. At dark—and it soon gets very dark in these regions, in spite of the grand stars which shine lustrously on us in a way of which no untravelled Englishman can form any adequate idea—we are on the Red Sea, having just passed the wreck of a steamer, as if to remind us that even in these days of science there are accidents arising from fogs and currents and hidden rocks and shoals which it is hard for any human ingenuity to guard against. Just now a good deal of interest attaches to the Red Sea. On our right are Suakim and Massowah, though too far off to be visible. Small as the Red Sea looks on the map, it is 1,200 miles long. Coral reefs and islands are so numerous that navigation is difficult and dangerous. The coast on either side seems deserted, and only now and then a lighthouse is to be seen, or the black hull of some small Arabian trader, with the well-known enormous sail from the yard-arm. However, there are one or two ports of importance on either side. The chief of all is Jeddah—with a population of 40,000—which is the port of the Mecca pilgrims, and which beside is the chief market for pearls and the black coffee and aromatic spices from Araby the Blest. Not far off is Mocha, a name familiar to British ears, though the place itself has fallen into decay.

So far as we have travelled the Red Sea has behaved uncommonly well. On the last voyage the heat was so intense that three times the ship had to be turned in order that the passengers might have a breath of cool air. As it is, no one finds the heat overpowering, and to me it yields the same amount of enjoyment one feels in a Turkish bath after the sweating process has got into full swing. We have little walking now except in the early morning, or after dark, and no gymnastic exercise of any kind. The little ones have already lost their rosy cheeks. Sunday is well observed; one way or another there is a good deal of preaching going on. The bishop takes in hand the first-class passengers, while in the evening volunteer preachers look after the souls of the second class. There was a special service also in the steerage in the afternoon, when the singing was at any rate very hearty.

Of course we gaze with no little pleasure at the island of Perim, standing in the deep water a few miles before we reach Aden. The French would have had it, the story goes, had not the Governor of Aden, who had his suspicions aroused as the French commander, who was sent to plant there the French flag, sat drinking champagne at his hospitable board, sent two notes, one to the harbour-master ordering him to delay the coaling, and another to the commander of a gunboat to sail at once with some artillerymen for Perim Such is the story as told by Sir Charles Dilke and other clever men; but the real fact is that it had been long before taken possession of by the old East India Company. At any rate, it is of no use to our French neighbours, now that they have lost Egypt, and that the control of the Canal has passed into English hands. Now the French have no Eastern Question. How we must all envy them!

In a little while we are out of the Red Sea, which at this time of year is really agreeable. All day long we have had a strong head wind, which has rendered the sultry atmosphere quite cool and genial. Provided an invalid is a good sailor, I should say, as far as we have gone, it would be impossible for him to have a more agreeable trip, or one more likely to return him to his native land of fog and frost and rain a better man. Everyone tells me that I am looking wonderfully better for my voyage. I am glad to hear it, as what is sauce for the goose is sauce for the gander, and I write in the hope that those who can afford it will follow in my steps. I have offered myself as an experiment for the sake of my asthmatic and elderly friends. So far as I have gone the experiment has succeeded beyond my most sanguine expectations.

We made rather a long stay at Aden, where most of the party went ashore; I did not, for of two evils a wise man chooses the least, and it seemed to me a greater evil to be rowed ashore and landed on a sunburnt rock where no water is than to fight with the coal-dust on board and to listen to the perpetual chattering of the natives. We have to be thankful that we are safe out of the Red Sea, which is certainly, with its sunken coral reefs and ragged rocks rising straight out of the water, as difficult a piece of navigation as any of which I ever heard. A captain had need be careful. The sights of Aden are few—a low building or two on the rocks, a native town a few miles off (not worth seeing), and water-tanks more useful than picturesque. Before we had anchored the Somali boys rowed round us in their little cockleshell boats, ready to dive for any coin thrown into the water. Then came the barges, black with coal, with long, dark, lightly-dressed natives, to convey the desirable mineral on board. Their woolly heads seem impervious to the sun's rays, and if they have dark skins, it but enhances the effect of their glistening teeth. The costume I like best is that of the native policeman, which consists of what looks to me like a nightgown, a turban, and a black necklace. A couple of gentlemen come on board: they wear blue jackets and rich-coloured silk skirts. Their hair is done up in a knot behind, and is kept in good order in front by a tortoise-shell comb. A few salesmen, with ostrich-feathers or wicker baskets, come to do a little business, but overboard the battle rages all day long, as the boys clamour for coins and imploringly stretch their skinny arms to the upper deck. A coin is tossed into the water: in a second they turn heels over head and disappear, in another second they have found it and are ready for another. The boats which take the passengers on shore are large, and manned by four or five men dressed in blue cotton. The charge is a shilling each way. The landing is easy enough, but in this hot climate I question whether a visit repays the trouble. Most of the passengers, however, seem to be of a contrary opinion ; nor is that to be wondered at when I state that many of them are ladies—or in other words, true daughters of Eve. They drive out to the tanks, and come back with headache and ears aching as well. In the meanwhile the row on board is incessant, as the wild Arabs of the sea scream for coins and perform all sorts of wonderful tricks in the way of diving. From the deck the scene is interesting and animated. Aden, with its brown rocks, is on our right : and ahead and on the other side of the bay runs the yellow sand, terminating—as everything does, apparently, on this rugged coast—in a peak of rocks. It is only the rock that belongs to us, and what we see are the offices of the company and the residence of the officials. The town is a terrible place to live in. On your way to the old town you meet endless strings of camels with the produce of the country, as in Aden itself not a blade of grass grows. The harbour is alive with ships, and steam-tugs towing the barges laden with coal, and native boats. Over the water seagulls and a bigger bird, apparently a kind of hawk, fly ceaselessly in search of their prey, and beneath sharks abound, as a white man would soon find to his cost were he to attempt a swim. Apparently the shark prefers the white man to the black, and there I and the shark agree. Away from Aden, which looks charming in the warm light of the setting sun, we pass out to the Indian Ocean, and the transition is a relief, as we leave behind the perpetual jabber of the natives of that fortunate district—I write fortunate advisedly, for the English spend a mint of money there, and the natives, to their credit be it written, know how to charge. In one particular case which came under my knowledge £2 was asked for an article for which ultimately the seller was content with 2s. We were to have had an addition to our live cargo in the shape of a smart little lad, whom an Australian had engaged to accompany him. The father was willing, but the brother, a fine-looking darkey, objected, and the boy was taken off again, apparently much against his will. I am told that many of these lads are taken away—they are apprenticed to the white man for a term of three years, the white employer agreeing to pay £12 a year in the shape of wages. As boys, they seem as active as monkeys. Whilst I was watching, one of them had his boat filled with water. In a moment he was out, and, rocking the boat till it was free from water, he paddled away with his one oar as if an upset in the water was an everyday occurrence; and the men seemed as agile as the boys—tall and muscular, with long arms and legs, and without an ounce of spare flesh. I fear by the side of them our Thames watermen would have but a poor chance.

Our captain tells me he can take a holiday now for the next few days. Out on the broad expanse of the Indian Ocean we are away from sunken rocks and coral reefs. According to Mr. Froude, when he made his way to Australia, he seems to have got through a good deal of Greek and Latin. In this delicious climate study of any kind seems quite out of place; but the sea air makes one hungry and indolent. We live well, and we have a library, which yields me a novel a day—of course I skip the descriptive parts and the sentimental—and as we rush over the blue sea, a cooling breeze meets us, and it is enough to live. I feel as if I were Ulysses and Christopher Columbus and Captain Cook rolled into one. We see no land, no ships, no birds in the heavens above, no fish in the water beneath. Night comes with its clear stars and its dark waves, and our pace is still the same. It is very wonderful, and none the less so that it is a wonder of everyday occurrence. Over the ship, in all parts, we have a perfect blaze of light—nine miles of electric wire! and outside all is darkness and mystery—a darkness and a mystery man has learned to master. Science has done that much for him. Will science unveil the darkness and mystery of being in a similar manner? I fear not. Happily there is a Judge

> Who ends the strife
> Where wit and reason fail.

CHAPTER III.

COLOMBO TO ALBANY.

Prosperity of Colombo—Native Extortioners—Buddhist Temple—Life in the Streets—On the Indian Ocean—Stormy Seas guard Australia—English Coolness—Western Australia.

A SCENE of Oriental loveliness opens on my dazzled eyes this morning. On my right is a fine breakwater, with a lighthouse at the end, which altogether cost £650,000, and the building of which occupied ten years. In front of me is the port of Colombo, filled with shipping from every quarter of the world. On my left is a long row of cocoa-palms, looking refreshing and green after the weary waste of waters we have travelled over. As I write the catamarans of Ceylon begin to crowd around. They are long, narrow boats—a stout Englishman would find it hard to sit in one of them—rowed by dusky sailors, with long oars, many of which seem to terminate in a sort of spade. The men are naked, with the exception of a cloth round the loins, and are apparently strong and sinewy. A few feet off is the outrigger, so formed that the boat never upsets. They may be useful, these boats, but have an awkward appearance to an English eye. They bring on board the men who have come to fetch the washing for the passengers, which will all be finished and on board before we leave. Then come the tailors, who will measure you for a suit of white, which will also be finished ere we depart. Then come the barges with the coal, and I get into a tug and go on shore. We all do it, for the *Orizaba* is unbearable while the coal is being put on board.

It is strange to remember that at one time Colombo was so far off, that the news of her Majesty's accession to the crown, which occurred on June 20, 1833, did not reach Colombo till some immense time after. Ceylon was between ninety and a hundred days from England, now it is only eighteen. Long after Lieutenant Waghorn had opened up the overland route, her Majesty's Government with characteristic stupidity still continued to send the mails by the Cape of Good Hope. It was left to the opening of the Suez Canal to render Ceylon easy of access, and to render it possible for English men and women to live there with comfort and luxury, in my humble opinion, far superior to anything we have at home, and Ceylon is redolent of prosperity, whether we regard its population, its revenue, or its trade. Directly the traveller lands at Colombo he feels as if in an enchanted isle.

As soon as you land in Colombo you are in India, and in, perhaps, its most attractive part. There are some 130,000 people in the city, all mild and gentle, and well-behaved. At once you are attracted by the grand Oriental Hotel, which faces the port ; you pass on a few steps, and come to lofty shops, filled with all the dazzling products of the East, with gardens in the rear, and it is hard to avoid being taken in, for the swarthy shopkeepers are clamorous, and, in the matter of cheating, quite the equal of the Heathen Chinee. A friend of mine purchases a white sapphire, as it is called, for eighteenpence, for which the owner asked four pounds, and I much fear my friend has been victimized after all. An unfortunate gentleman shows me a gold ring for which more than three pounds was paid, and which turns out not to be worth a halfpenny. But it is too hot to walk and I hire a carriage, and, with a companion, take a ride of a couple of hours for the small charge of three shillings. We start for the Buddhist temple, a whitewashed building about a couple of miles off. Externally there is little to see. It stands in a green court, surrounded by white walls, and the schoolmaster, after we have dropped a shilling into the box, and given him a trifle for himself, takes us round. The place consists of three courts, but the light is bad, and the schoolmaster's English very defective, and I came back little wiser than when I entered. The things that principally impressed me were a recumbent gigantic image of Buddha, a court in which there were seventy-five painted images of Buddha, and a smaller one in alabaster, and a long wall covered with representations of Buddhist legends which the schoolmaster, alas! did not condescend to explain. The Buddhist temple is small, and the only sign of its being used are the flowers scattered before the images, the offerings of his followers. The Christians, at any rate, make a good show as far as buildings are concerned, the Church of England heading the list with Christ Church Cathedral and nine other churches. The Presbyterians have two, the Wesleyans six, the Baptists one, the handsomest place of worship in the town, to say nothing of the Salvation Army, which has also a station here. Some people argue that Buddhism is such an exalted form of worship that we ought not to interfere with the faith of the people. That, however, is not the feeling of the whites in Ceylon, who know Buddhism best. To myself, with all my sympathy for Buddhism, the

Buddhist temple seemed a very poor affair. I should have said there are also many Mohammedans, and their mosques are numerous.

The streets are an endless delight, as you pass ladies riding in little hooded chairs on wheels, drawn by men; or swells, native or English, in broughams with latticed sides, so as to admit the breeze; and cars, rather rickety, drawn by native ponies and driven by native drivers, whom you may trust to take you to all the objects of interest to be seen, such as the hotels, the gardens, the museum, etc. Then there are native waggons, thatched with dried leaves, and drawn by little dun-coloured bulls with humps on their backs—active animals, which trot along with a swiftness of which a Sussex farmer, who still ploughs with oxen as his fathers before him, can have no idea. Under the trees you see the natives sitting over their dirty rice, which they still eat with unwashed hands. Where the natives live the population is almost as dense as in the East-end of London; and as to the pickaninnies, they are everywhere, with their little curly heads, sparkling eyes, and half-naked bodies, their mothers, in coloured dresses, leaving them pretty much to take care of themselves. Boys and girls run after us all the way with flowers, or bright beetles, or packets of cinnamon and other woods. All is strange, and all is attractive—the gorgeous butterflies that flit in the sun, the crowded streets, the native dwellings, with a screen of lath, which apparently does duty for a door; the tempting bungalows, standing in the midst of gardens with Oriental flowers, or under the shade of palm-trees, of which we in England can only dream; the grand promenades, where the residents walk of an evening to catch the refreshing sea-breeze; and the handsome parks, where English bands play English airs to the delighted crowds. The town is prosperous, undoubtedly. There are fine English barracks, and England's martial sons are to be met with everywhere. The whole island prospers under English rule. Ceylon's staple products—tea, coffee, and cinchona—employ hundreds of men, women, and children of different classes, and now an attempt is being made to introduce fish-curing. I could almost envy Arabi his place of banishment. I felt inclined to say with the poet, if there be an Elysium on earth, it is this; but then I was there in the cool time of year, when life is enjoyable, and when even the white man has a little of his native colour left. Yet even enchanting Colombo (I did not realize Heber's Ceylon's spicy breezes, quite the reverse, but perhaps that was my misfortune rather than my fault) has its drawbacks. As I am standing opposite the hotel, a native approaches with a small basket. He puts the basket on the ground and begins to pipe. To my horror, as he does so, a hooded cobra, lying *perdu*, with its black eyes and silver hood, erects itself on its tail as if ready to dart on its prey. Now, as above all things I hate snakes, and cobras most of all, I fled the spot and at once made for the tug, leaving the native juggler, I doubt not, not a little astonished at my want of taste.

Life on the ocean wave is really to be enjoyed on the Indian Ocean—an immense water, pleasanter to look at and sail on than the Atlantic, of which no one is sure, and which is variable as woman herself. It is impossible to overrate the beauty of the azure waves and skies which greet us every day. Nevertheless, we may have too much of a good thing, and no one regrets that we are approaching the end of our journey. At church on Sunday it seemed to me that we are much given to the use of misleading language. It was announced that the bishop would hold divine service, and perhaps he did so; at any rate, the assembly was numerous, and in appearance devout; but I missed the firemen who kept up the steam, the men on the outlook, the steersman on the bridge, and the inmates of the room set apart for the due study of charts. Were they not engaged in a service equally divine?

Colombo to Albany.

How, one by one, vanish the illusions of youth! Yesterday I would have sworn mangoes were delicious eating, for I have read so a thousand times; but to-day I have discovered the much-talked-of mango to be an impostor, in shape like a potato, with a great stone inside, only to be thrown away. Then what raptures we hear about the Southern Cross! I have seen it and it charms no longer, and the beauty of it is that the Australians who most rejoice in it seem utterly unable to tell you in what part of the heavens it shines. Then take the tropics. What descriptions one reads of tropical heats: heats fraught with deadly fever—heats so intense that an old man may well shrink from the danger of encountering them! I have been now nearly a week in the tropics, and they are really delightful. It is true you are warm; it is true that when the ports are closed by night the atmosphere in the cabin is apt to be unpleasant—but then that is of rare occurrence—and the tropics, I hold, so far from deserving to be run down, are favourably to be compared with London fogs and cold. We have now crossed the line, and have sailed for days along the Indian Ocean. Not a drop of rain has fallen on the deck, not a touch of bronchitis is to be met with in anyone aboard, not a ripple is to be seen on the great blue plain of the sea save that made by the *Orizaba* as she ploughs her majestic way at the rate of 320 miles a day. I should say, as far as my experience goes, any elderly man or woman, who in London suffers from its uncertain climate, would find the atmosphere of the Indian Ocean an immense change for the better. If any such require a real sanatorium, I would conscientiously recommend them a trip to Australia and back, if they can stand the sea, and if they have the good luck to secure a berth in such a ship as the *Orizaba*. By all means let them have a chair; I did not take one, as I thought it would not be worth the trouble, and even at Naples, when an ex-M.P. who went ashore there kindly offered me his chair as a parting gift, I had not sense enough to avail myself of the offer; but I have regretted it ever since. People who have chairs put them in the best places, where the breeze is most grateful, and thus enjoy a great advantage over those who can do nothing of the kind. By all means also let the tourist have a white dress; it is the only kind of dress to be tolerated on the Indian Ocean, and, of course, he must have canvas shoes, which he will find the more useful if they are soled with indiarubber rather than leather. You are bound to take as much exercise as you can, and it is not pleasant to fall on a slippery deck.

Let the intending traveller choose, if he can, his time. Between November and March the ocean is delightful. If, however, it is entered between May and September, when the thick weather and fierce winds of the south-west monsoon prevail, it is very much the reverse. It is a run of more than 3,000 miles from Colombo to Cape Leuwin, the south-west point of Australia, and this is the most monotonous part of the journey, as there is nothing to be seen on the sea. We only met two ships after leaving Colombo, and people grow sleepy and dull, and the conversation, at no time brilliant, rather flags. One can scarcely imagine what the horror of the passage was in not very remote times. When the bishop first went, he tells me, it was in a sailing vessel, and they were three months on the voyage, revelling on salt pork and beef all the while. Our modern bishops don't care much for that sort of diet, nor, if I may judge by the way we live, their flocks either, and this, by the way, is the real difficulty and danger on ship-board. As a rule, people are ill because they eat and drink too much. I have been a teetotaler all the while and have tried to eat as little as I could, and hence I am at any rate as well as anyone aboard. Again, let me caution the traveller to avoid a ship that rolls. In this respect we are wonderfully fortunate. The

Orizaba never rolls, and in the worst weather we dine in comfort, no crockery is smashed, and no steward spills a drop of soup. In the dark watches of the night it is the rolling that keeps passengers wide awake, and if ships can be built like ours it is a shame to send people on such long voyages in any others. In the tropics the clouds that come up as the fiery sun sinks into the blue sea are awful, darker and more threatening than any I have seen elsewhere. Then they disappear, and then again reappear, to fly with the early dawn. It is a long time before one can be reconciled to their grandeur. I am not surprised that people feel timid. There is a good deal to make people nervous at sea. A lady passenger tells me that when she goes to bed in rough weather, every night she expects to go to the bottom. I gave her what comfort I could; but then, as Festus grandly tells us, we live by heart-throbs not by years, and so the poor woman is to be pitied after all.

Not in summer calm, not when the gentleness of heaven is on the sea, do we approach the Australian coast. The garden of the Hesperides was guarded by dragons; and approach the Australian continent, for such it really is, which way you will, you find her defended by winds that are ever howling and seas that never are at rest. They did their best to frighten us as we made for the point where first we greet the granite rocks of the Land of the Golden Fleece; of course, there is no danger, and everyone pretends to enjoy it. As to myself, I frankly own—in spite of Byron and dear old Captain Basil Hall, whose pictures of sea-life, when I was in jackets, made everyone long to be a sailor—that I prefer calm to storm, and that never do I love the ocean so much as when it has ceased to roar. There are people who feel otherwise, just as there are people who enjoy the bagpipes, but they are the exception rather than the rule. It may be that the danger is little, but the motion of any ship on a stormy sea is unpleasant. It is to be questioned, however, whether there is any other sea-voyage so long, and at the same time attended with so little inconvenience, as this Australian trip, and I can quite understand how ready the Australians are to run 'home,' as they call it. They love Old England to the very bottom of their hearts. Some of them are quite ready to return and leave their bones amongst us. But we drive them away. One of my companions, for instance, has been spending a few weeks in London. He is a lawyer, and has made a lot of money, gotten chiefly at Ballarat in the good old times, when, instead of the ordinary six-and-eight, he always pocketed a fiver. It was his intention to have bought an estate and settled in England; but then it occurred to him that if he did no one would ever come to see him—at any rate, such was the universal testimony of those of his friends who had settled down in the old country, one of them a gentleman who had done the State some service and who had been presented at Court; and so my friend returns to Australia—swearing he will never go to London again—where he seems to have spent his money like a Nabob. Another complaint which I hear in many quarters is that Englishmen are ungrateful. One gentleman tells me how he had exerted himself on behalf of a young lad who had come out to Melbourne friendless, did all he could for him, treated him, in fact, as his own son, even had a gushing letter of thanks and gratitude from the mother, and yet when he called upon her in London she did not take the slightest notice of him; and in another case, where he introduced himself to the father of two young men to whom he had been the means of rendering much assistance, and to whom he had extended the utmost hospitality, all he received was a formal invitation to call when that way, and that only after he had met the grateful parent twice in the streets of the county town near which he lived. Colonials who have been hospitable to English visitors naturally expect a return of hospitality when they find themselves strangers in a strange land; and Englishmen should remember that it is at all times a duty to perpetuate the traditions of old English hospitality, and to take in the stranger in the Scriptural rather than in the modern way.

At length I have seen an albatross, and that may be taken as an indication that we are getting near our journey's end. It is a large bird, as big almost as a turkey, with white body and dark wings, but not often to be seen at this season of the year. For awhile we skirted the Australian coast, and dropped some thirty passengers for Western Australia at Albany, its chief port. They were sent ashore in a tug in rather a primitive fashion, and we had plenty of time to admire the magnificent harbour surrounded by granite rocks, enclosing a wide expanse of water, which we enter between two rocks, on one of which is a lighthouse. Of human habitations we saw nothing save one or two on the brow of a hill, at the bottom of which has been built a long railway pier, which railway, as it is not complete, is only used once a week, when the steamers arrive, for the purpose of conveying mails and passengers to Perth. 'I suppose the first port you touched at was Perth?' said an English M.P. and distinguished educationalist to me. Alas! it would have been hard work to have taken the *Orizaba* to Perth. Perth is the capital of a country eight times as large as the United Kingdom, which is at present a Crown colony, but which is to be made directly the home of a self-governing community. We dropped at Albany a young man who has been sheep-farming there for fifteen years, and is quite satisfied with the result. You could hardly credit how many thousand acres he has hired of the Government at a rental of 10s. a thousand acres. He has no white neighbours, and his labourers are chiefly native blacks, with whom, he tells me, he gets on very well. The country, he says, is well fitted for agricultural purposes, and there is plenty of good land to be bought at 10s. an acre. Hitherto the difficulty has been how to dispose of the produce, but that will shortly cease, as the district is now being opened up by railways, and from all that I can hear it is just the country for the British farmer who feels inclined to clear off before he has lost his last farthing in the vain attempt to compete with the foreign producer. In Western Australia, with a little capital, he may certainly do well. Everyone says Western Australia is the country of the future. As to Albany itself, it is growing rapidly, and has a population now of about 2,000. It seems to me prettily situated, and already people who have made a little money have fixed upon it as their residence. There are Church of England, Wesleyan, and Presbyterian churches there, and it boasts a paper—published weekly for threepence, and dear at the money—which found a large sale on board, for the sake mainly of its meagre telegraphic intelligence relating to English and European affairs. After the dreary monotony of the sea it was pleasant to look on the hills which hid Albany and its surrounding district from the vulgar gaze. On one hill there was a long trail of smoke, which indicated that somewhere there was a large bush fire; and climbing up the sides of all was a scanty undergrowth, which if good for neither man nor beast, had an appearance of verdure, which, to the eye, seemed a living green, now and then varied by stretches of yellow or white sand; and behind, though not visible to us from the deck of the steamer, stretched a forest, full of a black wood which makes the finest railway-sleepers in the world. On the whole, it may be said Western Australia is bound to go ahead.

CHAPTER IV.

IN THE COLONY OF VICTORIA.

Melbourne Gleanings—Dr. Bevan—Night at a Bungalow—Cole's Book-shop—A Day at Sorrento—White Cruelty to the Aborigines—Coffee Palaces—Dr. Strong—The Presbyterian Church in Collins Street—The Late Peter Lalor—Ballarat—Romance of Gold Mining—Sydney and Melbourne compared—Australian Rogues—Suburban Melbourne—Victorian M.P.'s—Victorian Politics.

THE stranger who makes his first trip to Australia is not a little astonished by the extreme cold which greets him as he nears his destination. You hear so much of Australian heat that you are not a little astonished to find the nearer you get to your journey's end the colder it becomes. In the tropics we had all given up warm clothing, but as we reached Western Australia great-coats by day and blankets by night came into fashion. People were wrapped up as if we were on the coast of England rather than of Australia, and as to sleeping with the ports open, that was quite out of the question. This is an admirable provision of Nature. It gives us the advantage of having the body braced up before it encounters the formidable heat which, according to all accounts, awaits us on shore. Another thing that strikes a stranger, as he studies the papers from all parts of the country, is the extraordinary difference in the weather as recorded in different localities. For instance, I find at Sydney the weather is described as delightfully cool, while at Adelaide on the same day it is recorded as the hottest of the season. In one district I read how the rain has come down in a perfect deluge, whilst in another men and vegetables are dying from the want of water. At a town in Queensland, the heat is so intense that many are dying daily of sunstrokes, and the insurance agents have been telegraphed to not to effect any more insurances, whilst in another locality I read of a heavy fall of snow. The fact is, it is impossible to realize the size of the Australian continent, twenty-six times larger than Great Britain and Ireland, or the various kinds of weather to be met with, till you are on the continent itself.

A pleasant trip of a day and a half from Adelaide, most of which time was passed in sight of land, enabled us to reach Melbourne—marvellous Melbourne, as it has been called—in time to go on board the *Lusitania* and bid good-bye to Miss von Finkelstein, who is, she tells me, wonderfully delighted with her Australian trip, and intends returning again. She goes now as far as Port Said, and thence she makes her way to Jerusalem. I then get into the train, and after a run of half an hour along a flat district, partly waste and partly built over with little wooden villas—prettily painted, each with its tiny garden, which seemed to me to have a wonderful knack of getting burnt down every night—find myself landed in the noble thoroughfare, which seems to me to run from one end of the city to the other, known as Collins Street ; and almost the first person I meet—at any rate, the first one I recognise—is Dr. Hannay, who is leaving by the next mail steamer, and who is looking very well, though he tells me he has been much tried by the great heat of the last fortnight. The dust and the sun are trying, and I get back to the ship for dinner.

When next I go on shore it is Sunday morning, and a grateful breeze awaits me as I make my way along picturesque and stately Collins Street—a street which would be an ornament to London itself. The public-houses are closed, the tramcars have ceased running, and the busy crowds that block up the footways on the week-day are away. Instead of them there are the church-goers — well-dressed, sedate, orderly—just as we may see anywhere in England on the Sabbath. And if I miss the sound of the church-going bell, I know not that that is an unmitigated loss—indeed, as far as London is concerned in that respect, it always seems to me that we may have too much of a good thing. On my left I pass a handsome Baptist Church, which was crammed to suffocation when a short time since Rev. Dr. Maclaren, of Manchester, was preaching. Further on I pass the fine Scots Church, and on the other side of the crossing is the noble church of which Dr. Bevan is the popular pastor, and where I tarry to admire the cool and spacious structure, the appearance of the people, and the eloquence of the preacher. It is the premier church of Victoria, and is in every way worthy of its position. The people rejoice in an endowment of £3,700 a year, all of which is turned to good purposes, and they give at the doors as much as £1,500 a year, to say nothing of pew rents. It is not in Victoria that you feel doubts as to the power of the Churches to evangelize the land. Here, as all over the colonies, the Church of England leads the way, and—as was to be expected when you remember what an adventurous race of men the Scotch are—the Presbyterians occupy the second place. The Wesleyans and the Congregationalists come next, and of the latter body Dr. Bevan is the leader, and he seems to me to enjoy his position to the utmost. He is the picture of health and happiness, and, as I tell him, is to be likened rather to a wealthy archdeacon at home than to a Congregational minister, as we know him, in a country where he has to take — thanks to Parliamentary wisdom — rather a place in the second rank. He and Mrs. Bevan alike seem to have renewed their youth in this far-off land. A dealer in portraits of English celebrities, by-the-bye, tells me that people often ask him if the portrait of John Bright he displays is not that of the worthy Doctor. And, indeed, there is a breadth and vigour in the Doctor's sermons which naturally suggests to the hearer the fiery eloquence of John Bright. Standing in his gown, on his platform pulpit, the Doctor certainly carries all before him. His audience seems to be wielded at his will, and his audience is a noble one; men and women to whom the service of the sanctuary is not a form or conventional observance or symbol of respectability, but a joy and delight, which reminds one of what churchgoing was, in what to sceptical and scientific London seems a far-off time, when Dr. Watts could write:

> At once they sing, at once they pray,
> They hear of heaven and learn the way.

What strikes me as a contrast to congregations I know nearer home is the power of the audience. The people are in the prime of life, not decayed and elderly, and the proportion of young men is great. In the evening they make a grand show in the gallery —semi-circular, lofty, and airy. And this is, remember, the summer season, when families rush off to the seaside, and corresponds to the period when in London our churches are thin, and when in New York and Washington, and the other great centres of American life and energy, it is usual for the pastor to shut up his church, and for the people to give themselves a Sunday rest—not in the Jewish, but in the modern acceptation of that term. In the afternoon I enjoyed the hospitality of one of the Doctor's deacons, Mr. Johnson, who has had the honour of making his handsome house the temporary residence of Mr. Henry Lee, who is away preaching.

In every direction I look I see capacious streets with handsome houses, all painted white, and broad streets which are lined for miles with the dwellings of the Melbournites, while as you wander in wonder, every now and then, beyond the glitter of the white houses, and the green foliage of the public gardens, you see a thin silver streak of the blue bay. In the evening, the Doctor will have me go home with him.

We stop late, for there are people waiting to see the Doctor in his private vestry; then we catch the last tram to Camberwell—how funny the old name seems to us on this Australian soil! Then we are driven home by the Doctor's Jehu—who, I fancy, has rather a good time of it, though, as a Roman Catholic, he holds his master to be a heretic—and we have a welcome supper in a veritable bungalow, large, and occupying its own grounds of thirty acres, devoted by the Doctor to farming, on an interesting, but, I fear, rather unprofitable, scale. At an early hour on Monday morning—for we have much to talk of over our cigars, uncommonly fine ones, a present to the Doctor—I am offered a choice of beds, of course all on the ground-floor. I resolved to sleep in the one which has recently been tenanted by Dr. Hannay, of whom everyone in Melbourne speaks well. As the Doctor shows me to my bed and shuts down the window, I am idiot enough to say, 'Any snakes about here, Doctor?' 'Only a few black ones now and then,' he replies, in a light and airy way. But, alas! the Doctor's words kept me uncommonly wide awake that night.

One of the sights of Melbourne, the most marvellous I have yet seen, is that known as 'Cole's Book Arcade,' in Bourke Street, which is not merely a place for the dissemination of knowledge, useful or otherwise, but a reading-room as well, into which thousands enter, pick up a book, take a seat, and read as long as they like without spending a farthing. Mr. Cole himself, the owner, is a remarkable man. He hails from Ashford, in Kent, and had been some time in the colony trying to make a fortune, but with little success, and now evidently he has, to borrow an Americanism, 'struck ile.' As a compiler he has done some good work. His aim is to publish the Library of the Future, to be composed entirely of the cream of human thought and knowledge. To this scheme he gives the title of 'The Federation of the World's Library.' It is to consist of one hundred of the best books in the world; one book, the best of its kind, is to be on astronomy, another on geology, another on geography, and so on. Each book is to be complete of its kind, and highly condensed. It is easily and perfectly done, he says. A moderate-sized song-book, he tells us, holds all the best songs in the world; a moderate-sized wisdom-book—it is a humiliating reflection—will hold all the wisest sayings in the world; a moderate-sized book, carefully prepared, of astronomy, geology, chemistry, botany, or any of the sciences, will give a clear knowledge of the principles of each. Such a library, of 100 volumes of 600 pages each, can be produced to sell at £10, thus bringing all the most important knowledge and all the most beautiful thoughts within the reach of every human being. He calculates that there are a million printed poems in the world. The 1,000 best are worth the remaining 999,000 all put together. Probably out of the 1,000 best there are 100 first-class, 300 second-class, and 600 third-class. Amongst the first-class Mr. Cole reckons Gray's 'Elegy,' Goldsmith's 'Deserted Village,' and Longfellow's 'Psalm of Life.' As a bookseller he asserts—and I am sorry to write it— that it is read more, verse for verse, than the whole of Milton's and Homer's poems put together. Mr. Cole tells me that, with the exception of school books —always in demand—his principal sales are novels and theological works. Of the latter he sells most of Talmage. Ward Beecher does not go down so well. Perhaps the Australians in this respect resemble some of the members of the Christian Young Men's Association. When last in London, Mr. Cole went to hear the great American lecture at Exeter Hall. 'Mr. Beecher ought not to be allowed to lecture here,' said someone to him. 'Why so?' asked Mr. Cole. 'Because he is an infidel,' was the charitable reply.

And what a sight Mr. Cole's shop is, to be sure! especially at business hours, when it swarms with buyers and readers. It is three stories high, 200 feet deep, and 40 feet wide. Its walks are a third of a mile long, and its capacious galleries are supported by 140 brass pillars. The sign of the establishment is the rainbow, which is to be seen painted everywhere. A gorgeous rainbow ornaments the chief entrance in Bourke Street. Inside daily may be seen hundreds of men, women, and children, who really seem more numerous than they are in consequence of the seventy mirrors with which the interior is decorated. There are twenty miles of boards in the shelving, and 2,800 large cedar drawers. Altogether there are 100,000 sorts of books, all well classified, so that the purchaser can at once secure what he requires, and if he wants a selection he has probably a million of books to choose from. New books, music, and stationery occupy the ground-floor, second-hand books the next floor, and on the top floor is a fine collection of china, glass, and other house ornaments and knick-knacks. This flat is entirely devoted to the sale of goods to beautify the interiors of houses, as books beautify the mental interiors of their readers. If you want to get to the top, and you are too tired and weary to walk, there is a handsomely-decorated lift at your service, and if you require the solace of music there are free performances given every afternoon and evening. Mr. Cole, to his credit be it said, has prohibited, as far as he is concerned, the sale of Zola's novels, having struck them out of his list. I asked one of his *employés* to what religious body he belonged. I was amused with this reply : 'I don't know ; but he's a very good man. I expect he is a Dissenter.' It is curious to find people who do not go to Episcopalian churches spoken of as Dissenters in a land where there is no State Church, and where all denominations are on an equality ; but then this particular young man had only left the Old Country a year and a half, and had not got rid of his Old World ideas. As an illustration of the value of property in Melbourne, Mr. Cole tells me that his rent is £1,000 a year, that he has a lease of it for fifteen years, and that the proprietor nevertheless had had an offer made him for the place of £5,000 a year. All round Mr. Cole's premises are what he calls intellect sharpeners, in the shape of extracts from what wise men have written in favour of study and reading. This Australian Cole seems in his way to do much to advance Australia.

One of the few places in Australia to which interesting associations attach is Sorrento, and it is one of the places most patronised by the Melbourne public. You leave Melbourne Port at half-past eleven, and you arrive there at two. As the steamer returns at half-past three, you have not much time for exploration, and in my own case I admit that time was curtailed from perfectly natural causes. As I landed, the announcement 'hot dinners' met my eye, and gave me quite an appetite. I walked up the cliff, found a comfortable and airy hotel at the top, and did justice to a good half-crown dinner. Nor was I singular. I found many of my travelling companions similarly disposed. One must dine, and you may as well dine in comfort as not.

Everyone in Melbourne goes to Sorrento. I was in the former city on one of the days when the heat is tropical, when the hot wind and the dust are intolerable, when everyone in the city looks parched and weary; while the wives and mothers and daughters at home draw down the blinds, fasten all the doors to keep the hot air out, and sit metaphorically in dust and ashes. In vain are scanty attire and cooling drinks; in vain are all the resources of human ingenuity. The only thing to do is to take the train to Melbourne Port, and then get on board the steamer for Sorrento, where the temperature is always twenty degrees lower than in Melbourne. The wind blows straight from Port Melbourne to the Heads; it has no heated land to pass over on its way to Sorrento, and arrives there cool and bracing from its contact with the salt water. On one side we have the Bay, and on the other side the Southern Ocean, only a narrow mile of land dividing them. It has a charming locality all round, picturesque cliffs, and the sea. Traces of the old settlement are visible still. One of the original wells sunk in 1803 has been opened for the use of the public, and the shade of the scrub gives special advantage to picnic parties, for which the whole picturesque extent of country round is admirably adapted. It was here came the original settlers. One of the oldest, just carried to his last long home, used to tell terrible stories of them. 'Had you any trouble with the natives in those days?' asked an anxious inquirer. 'Trouble!' was the reply; 'not me, poor things. Why, sir, they were as harmless as babies. I have seen upwards of a thousand on 'em at a corroborree on the Meni creek —that was their camping-ground then. Dear, dear, poor things, they're gone now, sir, gone; most on 'em shot off, or put out of the way somehow else. If there is any questions asked when we are dead and gone, some of our big squatting swells ull have some awful posers to answer.' Again, added the old man, 'Take my word for it, sir, the blacks were a harmless, good-natured lot till the cruelty of the whites made 'em bad and revengeful, poor things; and who can blame 'em?' The flour which they used was mixed with arsenic, and thus they lost in many cases their lives and lands. In one case it was certain that a native was shot by a celebrated *savant* that he might have possession of the native's skull. There are few natives left now. Such humane treatment has somewhat diminished their number. At all times it was a puzzle what to do with them, as the following well-authenticated anecdote shows. Two aboriginal children, separated from babyhood from aboriginal life, were trained and educated like colonists. In the earlier years little difference was noted, but as they advanced into boyhood, some restlessness became apparent. Ultimately, when a native tribe happened to come near, the children escaped, to taste once more the charms of savage life. The Australians employ many of them, and make them useful in many ways, but none of them rise to anything like a position in the social scale, or evince any capacity of ever rising to become more than hewers of wood and drawers of water. I have seen them usefully engaged at such places as the Point Macleay Mission, in South

Australia, but even there I question whether they earn their own living. On one occasion I crossed Lake Alexandrina in a sailing-boat managed by blacks, and I was not drowned—which, however, does not say much for their nautical skill, as the lake was as calm as a mill-pond.

But to return to Sorrento. The history of this place begins with the discovery of the fine harbour of Port Philip by Lieutenant Murray, a harbour of some forty miles in extent. The next year it was made the site of a convict settlement under Governor Collins, who soon had enough of the place, and started off for Tasmania. Eight convicts were missing within a month of their arrival. Four were brought back and punished, one was shot by a constable, and the three others, oppressed with hunger, after wandering round the western shores of Port Philip, made fires to attract the attention of their companions, but without success. Two of them walked back to surrender themselves into the hands of justice, but were never heard of after; and for a while the place was left to the kangaroos and the natives, till there arrived on the scene Hamilton Hume, a native-born colonist of New South Wales. In 1834 three gentlemen named Henty established a whaling station at Portland Bay, and this was the first settlement in Victoria. At this time, and for some time afterwards, the natives were easily beguiled. As late as 1835 a John Bateman, of Hobart Town, landed on the western shore of Port Philip, and entered into a contract with the natives for 1,000 square miles of territory for a few blankets to be given them every year. The Government refused to sanction this iniquitous transaction. Nevertheless, the natives were despoiled of their land—Governor Bourke annexed it in the name of his Majesty. Melbourne, on the Yarra, was named after the British Premier of that day, and Williamstown, where the grand boats of the Orient and P. and O. Companies land and embark their passengers, had the questionable honour of being named after our Sailor King.

Port Philip was a place rather given to joviality and adventure. Ladies and children were rare. There was a marvellous consumption of brandy. Manners, when visible, were rough. 'The town,' writes an old settler, 'was bad, and the bush was worse.' When a pious missionary of those early times, prior to adventuring into the interior, inquired of a squatter if the Sabbath was kept in the bush, 'Oh yes,' was the prompt reply; 'a clean shirt and a shave.' 'At the time of my arrival,' writes Mr. Westgarth, 'all Melbourne-bound passengers were put out by their respective ship's boats upon that part of the northern beach of Port Philip that was nearest to Melbourne, whence in struggling lines, as best they could, in hot winds, they trod a bush-path of their own making, which, about a mile and a half long, brought them to a punt or little boat just above the Falls—which they crossed for the small charge of threepence.' There are people who still maintain that Melbourne is planted on the wrong site, that Williamstown, with its healthful level, might have been better, or Geelong, with its beautiful ready-made harbour, and its direct access to all the superior capabilities of the West and North-west. The traveller, as he runs down to Sorrento by an excursion steamer, may, perhaps, agree with the critics. But, then, Sorrento would never have had a chance. Now it is a place to spend a happy day in, and many are the Melbournites who lodge in the vicinity. I would have tarried there longer, but steamers—like time and tide—wait for no man.

In one thing Melbourne beats London and all Australia put together, and that is in the number and excellence of its coffee-palaces, which are a real boon to the travelling public, and which may claim to have solved the question how, by co-operation, to provide homes of comfort and luxury for the great middle-class of the community. The Federal Coffee-Palace in Melbourne is a remarkable illustration of what may be done in this way. Instead of spending three or four pounds a week at an hotel, and being expected to injure my health for the benefit of my landlord, I pay half a crown for my bed—it is true it is high up on the sixth floor, but then I go up and down by the lift, which is in active operation from seven in the morning till midnight; I get a good breakfast in a handsome apartment, served up by attractive young maidens in neat black dresses, for which I pay one-and-threepence; I can have a good lunch for a shilling; and my evening meal, with fish or flesh, costs about the same sum. There is a café attached, in which I can have a cup of coffee or some light refreshment at any time; a reading-room, if I require it; a smoking-room, if I am given to that mild form of self-indulgence; and a billiard-room, if I require a little exercise after the worry of the day. As soon as I rise I have a comfortable bath, which is not an extra, as in England. Nor need I fear being roasted alive, as half a dozen watchmen perambulate the place all night. In England we have nothing of this kind. We have large and grand hotels, but they are utterly beyond the reach of persons of moderate means; and it is a question whether, in these days when it is hard to get a decent servant-girl, something after the plan of the Federal Palace at Melbourne might not be started in London and our other big cities, not as a rest for the comfort and delectation of the weary traveller, but as an associated home. It is only in that way that the increasing difficulties connected with houses and servants, and the cost of living in London, can be met and overcome. The servant-girl in these coffee-palaces is far superior to her sister who acts the part of maid-of-all-work in a London suburb. She is always civil, always well dressed, always ready to oblige. She knows when her work is over, and that is a great consideration. She has her day out when she is off duty, and that keeps her in good temper all the rest of the week. At all times her appearance and behaviour are respectable. I have always found her cheerful and pleasant, much given to devoting her spare time to novel-reading, which helps to keep alive romance in her heart and preserve her youth. It is evident she is not over-worked in the coffee-palace; she looks too well and flourishing. I hope she marries well, and lives happily ever after. It seems to me that she deserves a good husband and a good home.

On the Federal Coffee-Palace money has been spent with a liberal hand; and it is run by a company, who find it, I believe, a commercial success. All that is wanted is a little better management. Melbourne is a city of fine buildings, and the Federal may vie with any of them as regards external grandeur and internal accommodation. The freehold alone cost £48,000, and the building and furniture for 400 sleeping-apartments, to say nothing of the public rooms, must have cost at least £150,000 more. Its tower, which is 200 feet high, is a landmark from all quarters. The site is happily chosen, as the Federal is not only close to the terminus of the railways, but is likewise in close proximity to the wharves on the Yarra, which are now daily crowded with large and powerful steam-vessels engaged in inter-colonial and foreign trade. The Custom House is near at hand, and business-men and visitors can, by means of the cable tramways in front of the palace, be speedily conveyed to any of the city suburbs. It has a post and telegraph-office attached, and the popular firm of Thomas Cook and Son have an agency in connection with it. Collins Street, in which it stands, is the centre of trade and commerce. It is there all the great companies have their head-quarters, the papers are published, and all the wealth and fashion of the city congregates. The foundations of the new building, which enclose an area of half an acre, were laid at an expense of many thousands of pounds. The underground arrangements are admirable. One apartment is devoted entirely to pastry-cooks; in another is a freezing-apparatus, in which meat, poultry, and game may be kept fresh for a month or more. Another apartment is devoted to grills; and the kitchens are connected with the floors above them by several lifts, by which the cooked viands are noiselessly and rapidly raised to the various sitting-rooms, and the dishes so returned to the sculleries. As to the entrance, that must be seen to be appreciated—wide folding-doors open into a grand marble vestibule, which extends between massive columns into an interior hall. In the centre is the principal staircase, leading to the first-class dining-room and the upper stories. The area above is surrounded by galleries which serve as balconies, where the lady-visitors and their friends may be seen sitting all day long gazing on the busy crowd of arrivals and departures below. You may be almost said to sleep in marble halls, and the beauty of it is that all this splendour is not for the benefit of the bloated capitalist, but for the comfort of the many.

One Sunday I had rather a strange experience. I

went to the Presbyterian Church in Collins Street, where there was a large congregation to listen to a fine sermon by the reverend minister on the custom of the primitive Church to have all things in common—a custom which the orator conclusively showed to the satisfaction of his hearers, wealthy Scotchmen, with few leanings towards Socialism in any form, was quite exceptional, and was not to be dreamed of in these latter days. I had a pair of gloves, which I laid down in the pew. When half-way out of the church I recollected that I had left those gloves behind. I returned to look for them, mentioning the fact to the gentleman who sat next me. On rushing to where I sat I found a pair of gloves exactly similar to my own at the back of the pew, and, concluding that they were what I sought, returned in triumph. Just as I had got to the door a young man came and claimed the gloves—and I gave them up—when, to my amazement, the same gentleman (?) who had sat in the pew with me, and to whom I had mentioned the loss of my gloves, handed my own over to me. It is true that the sermon was about having all things in common, but I object to such a practical application.

In Melbourne Dr. Strong, who was expelled from the Scotch church to which I have already referred, is making the experiment of carrying on a church without a creed. Apparently the attempt is a successful one. When I attended the congregation was a large one, and the sermon very interesting. It is a fine building in which they meet, and the people seem to be highly respectable, as much so as I have seen anywhere. Dr. Strong calls his place 'The Australian Church.' It seems to me, as far as I can make out, that the wish is father to the thought. I see no evidence in Australia that the people are discontented with the old ways, or are ready for change. Men immersed in business and money-making as a rule do not affect heresy; they are mostly conservative in politics and religion. From what I hear, it is the personal influence of Dr. Strong that has built the church and filled it. He is very popular with his people. They followed him from his old church to his new one, but they are not fanatics in favour of their new denomination, and I question whether out of Melbourne there is sufficient population to be developed into anything worthy to take the somewhat ambitious title of the Australian Church. The Wesleyans, the Presbyterians, and the Church of England, have already gone up and taken possession of the land, and they are organized, which is half the battle. 'Our people,' said a colonial bishop to me one day, 'are not likely to be caught by the Salvation Army.' The Church has its own organization, and it is that which keeps the flock from wandering. As long as they get something in the way of religious worship they are content. People who belong to other bodies tell me that the Church of England parsons are poor preachers, that they are, many of them, men who have failed in other pulpits, or who have been unable to pass the requisite examination, or whose characters do not stand high—and certainly I have seen some queer specimens of the genus. But then, says the devout worshipper, 'we go to church to pray and to worship God. The sermon is not the main thing with us, as it is amongst the other religious bodies.' It may be that he is wrong—I am not about to contest that matter—but it seems to me that in Melbourne the better preacher the man is the better does his church fill; and that if the Church of England, or any other religious body, seeks to be successful, due care must be taken that there is life in the pulpit. The stranger would think Melbourne a very religious city; much more so than London, or any town or city at home. The public-houses are strictly closed; the trains do not run till two o'clock. There is no Sunday newspaper published (in Sydney there are two, and both pay well). Except for the well-dressed crowds on their way to their favourite church (they are all churches here—Little Bethels and Mount Zions are unknown), and the church bell, you would think such places as Sydney and Melbourne on a Sunday morning the cities of the dead. Walking along Bourke Street one Sunday evening—a street always black with pedestrians at that time—I saw a crowd hanging about the door of a theatre. I went in and found a place full of real working men in their working attire, who had come to enjoy a religious discussion. I got in only at the end, and heard but the orthodox reply from a gentleman who talked a good deal about matter and space, and the operations of the one great God, who had revealed Himself to man in the person of Jesus Christ. The crowd sat listening patiently till nine o'clock, when the gas was turned off, and they lit their pipes and went home. I heard some speaking of the objector, whom I was too late to hear, as a very clever fellow; but the mass seemed quite indifferent. I spoke to one or two of the hearers, whose minds seemed a perfect blank. There was no praying, no singing, no attempt to attract, no pale youth with a concertina, no tender maiden to sing a solo. In London the thing would have been a failure. Here the working man has his beershop and club, and his penny paper.

In Australia he has nothing of the kind, and he is open to conviction even if it comes to him in a secularist form.

There has lately passed away a man well known in Victoria as Peter Lalor. He was an Irishman, and lived to be Speaker of the Victorian Parliament; but it was as a revolutionist that he gained his true fame. When the news of the discovery of gold in Ballarat filled that district with seekers from every part of the world, Mr. Peter Lalor was one of the first to put in an appearance. Melbourne and Geelong were almost emptied of their male inhabitants. Government was at its wit's end how to preserve order among the young community. In 1855, the Government promulgated the right of the Crown to the gold, and issued licenses to the diggers. With a view to keep back the crowd, the license fee was increased from £1 10s. to £3 a month. This was more than the hardy gold-diggers could stand. They were not represented in Parliament, and they took the law into their own hands after their patience had been exhausted by the insults of the martinets in office, who were sent to see that they had all the requisite licenses, and to whom hunting the diggers was a pleasant sport. The Gold Commissioners, as they were called, were frequently corrupt, and always insolent and overbearing. At length matters came to a crisis. A digger got killed in a house that did not bear a good character, and the landlord was considered to have been a participator in the murder. The man was tried with others, and discharged. In their indignation over the untimely end of a chum, the diggers subscribed, and had a new trial. It was while holding a meeting for this purpose that they came into collision with the police, who were guarding the hotel. The place was burnt down, and three of the incendiaries were imprisoned. Another meeting was then held to demand the release of the prisoners, and at the same time to claim manhood suffrage, and other political and social reforms. Soon, losing all confidence in the Government, they began to drill and arm. Fighting commenced in real earnest under the flag of the Southern Cross. They were attacked, and amongst the wounded was their general, the late Speaker, Peter Lalor. The eyes of the blind were opened. Government, in time, learned to act rationally, and the result was, Ballarat became the centre of a law-abiding people—a people, nevertheless, given over to the worship of the golden calf. 'I remember it,' said a man to me yesterday, as I wandered along its streets, down which a whirlwind of white dust was unpleasantly blowing, 'when there was only one house in the town; when it was all gum-trees and tents. There,' said he, pointing to a particular spot at the entrance of the town—'is where the Welcome Nugget was found; it was worth £5,000, and was discovered by a couple of diggers who had barely been earning their living for months. There,' he continued, 'I had a miner's right; I sold it for £50 to the present owner, of whom a syndicate has been trying to buy it for £40,000. Them was hard times. I remember when I walked twelve miles to a store, and could only bring back a pound of butter, and that was a favour.' But most of the miners lost their money as quickly as they made it. 'In 1860,' he added, 'I was ready to go home, but in 1861 I was up a tree.'

Ballarat has now settled down into a rather humdrum sort of city, with a population of about 50,000. The diggers are mostly dead or gone, and few traces of them remain, save in the turned-up earth outside the town, where there are traces still remaining of what they called shallow digging. On a hill just outside, also, it is evident that there has been a good deal of soil turned up, or turned out, in the search for gold, but no alluvial deposits exist; gold, if found, is only found in quartz, and that has to be crushed, and the gold eliminated by machinery of a very complicated and costly character, to secure which a company has to be formed, and then the returns, in the shape of dividends, are generally small. It is unhealthy work, too, in the mines, and I was not surprised to find that many of the men had left, and taken to farming instead. Any morning in the week you will find a lot of agents and brokers in the Ballarat Mining Exchange, ready to do a little business in the way of speculation, and that is, perhaps, all that remains to testify as to what Ballarat was in its golden age. As to the riotous living of the past, that is a matter of tradition. The fact is, Ballarat has had its day. Where the carcase is, there the eagles gather, and little of the carcase is left in Ballarat. Mount Morgan and Broken Hill are now names of greater power. Ballarat has an Episcopalian bishop. The Wesleyans and Presbyterians are very strong in the town. The Roman Catholics and the Congregationalists are also in evidence. Somehow or other I missed the Episcopalian place of worship; but with its schools and other buildings, with its wood warehouses and stores, I felt how great had been the change, how sober and quiet had become the Ballarat of to-day. 'We shall meet again, sir,' said my unknown friend, in a tone the honesty of which deeply affected me—' we shall meet again, sir, some day. Let us hope it will be in the right place.'

Of the romance of Ballarat one gets a good idea from a story which I found in a newspaper which will certainly interest the general reader. The history of one of the Ballarat claims, called the Blacksmith's Claim because its first owner belonged to this craft, reads like a page of romance. The blacksmith, with a party of eight, all novices, sank the shaft in so irregular and unworkmanlike a manner, that it was absolutely at the risk of his life that a man made the descent to the bottom. Without opening out a regular drive they washed all the stuff within reach, and after realising £12,800 offered it for sale, but so wet and rotten was the ground, so badly sunk the shaft, that at first no purchaser could be found. At last a party of ten plucked up courage and bought all right and title to the claim and tools for £77. They entered into possession at noon on Saturday, and long before the sun had set had in their possession £2,000 worth of gold. By working day and night in spells till the following Monday they raised this to £10,000. Then, after the usual reckless manner of lucky diggers, they left this mine of wealth, and went on the spree for a week. Their tenants made good use of the time at their disposal; they opened up two drives; and before the week was out were the happy possessors of £14,400, all taken out of the claim. The other party then returned, and after a week's work, during which they realized £9,000, they sold out to a storekeeper for £100, who put in a gang to work on shares, and these, labouring in a desultory fashion for a fortnight, took but £5,000. At the end of that time, one of the party, an old hand from Van Diemen's Land, undermined the props, and next morning on returning to work the men found the whole of the workings had fallen in. The rest of the party appeared to have taken this misfortune very calmly, and to have completely abandoned the claim, for no mention is made of their further proceedings; but it is related how the author of the mischief coolly marked out a claim 24 feet square on the top of the ruin, and working with a hired party, sunk a shaft straight as a die for the gutter. The first tubful of wash dirt they found turned out 40 lb. weight of gold, and the next two averaged 10 lb. each, and as Ballarat gold was and is superior to any other at all times, fetching at least £4 an ounce, those three bucketfuls of earth were worth £2,880 to their fortunate possessor. Altogether, out of that small area, hardly larger than a good-sized room, was taken in a few weeks gold worth nearly £30,000.

Round Ballarat the country is rather prettier than is the average of Australian scenery. All the way from Geelong, situated rather charmingly at the bend of a pretty bay, which is bound to become a fashionable watering-place, the land rises till you nearly reach Ballarat, when you go down a slight incline. The soil is good, and there are many twenty-acre farms, and the heat is not so great as in Melbourne. Out of the town there is a fine sheet of water, devoted to boating and black swans, and there is a botanical garden, in which I own I was somewhat disappointed, though everyone (perhaps it was for that very reason) said it was one of the places which I was bound to go and see, and which would delight me greatly. The Ballarat people, I was told in the train, were hospitable. It may be so, but I can bear no testimony on that point, as none of their hospitality was extended to me. My only experience of them was at an ordinary at the principal hotel, and there I was not particularly gratified, as conversation seemed quite out of the question. Now I come to think of it, that must have been through fear of the head waiter, who certainly was a very superior personage indeed, and was much better got up than any of his guests. Be this as it may, it was with little regret that I got on board the train and left the Golden City, with its green foliage, its red-brick houses, its white town-hall, its awful dust, its broad streets, and its rough pedestrians, far behind.

Anthony Trollope tells us that no one who has ever paid Sydney a visit will leave it without a tear or a regret. I confess I had no such feeling as I got into a hansom and drove down to the *Liguria*—a ship dear to many—which is to be known no more to Australian friends, as her destination henceforth is to be South America; but she took me safely to Melbourne, where I landed, to be more than ever charmed with the busy city and its people, a city and a people who believe themselves destined to the leadership of these sunny lands. Sydney is too old, they say, handsome as it is in parts, and Brisbane is too hot, to be in the running. As long as Sydney is faithful to Free Trade she will be a great emporium of commerce; but the democracy rule in Sydney, and the democracy all the world over have lost faith in Free Trade. Sydney has little to boast of besides its unrivalled harbour, lined with health resorts where wealth, and beauty, and fashion congregate, and where all the residences are of the most captivating character—white villas with verandas, rising out of green lawns shaded by tropical plants, and gorgeous with tropical flowers, in bloom, at any rate, the greater part of the year—where the blue waves ever murmur underneath. I must own, too, that some of the shops in Sydney are far finer than any to be seen in Melbourne; and the post-office at Sydney is, perhaps, the noblest building of the kind to be seen anywhere. A similar remark applies to the Town Hall, completed after I left. But Melbourne has, in Collins Street, a unique and stately thoroughfare, such as can be seen nowhere else—a street as gay of an afternoon as Regent Street, and as difficult in crossing, owing to its swarming traffic, almost as Cheapside. Sydney has no such show; and the Melbourne ladies tell me that it is to that place that the Sydney drapers come for the latest fashions. It seems to me that there is a great deal more drinking in Sydney than in Melbourne. Almost every other house you come to is an hotel, and it has its bar, where, under the presidency of two or three rather showy damsels, the drinking goes on all day. In both cities there is apparently more drinking than in London, except in the poorest quarters, affected by the beggar, and the pauper, and the tramp, by depraved men, and women infinitely worse. But for Melbourne and Sydney a defence may be made which is not available at home. The population in both cities is of a very migratory character; a large number of men spend their time in passing from one colony to another, and in this way they make many acquaintances, and when they meet they have a drink. In Sydney the fashion is to hand you the bottle and let you help yourself. The landlord finds it to his interest to do so. The customer takes less than the landlord would give him for his sixpence. The customer knows that he has the day before him, and that it will not do to get exhilarated too soon. There are drinks awaiting him with other friends at other bars and at other hours, and so he takes as little whisky as he can in his glass. Superficially, Melbourne seems the more moral town, but so far as my experience goes all cities are much alike. Chicago proudly boasts that it is the wickedest city in the world, but I much doubt its claim to that bad pre-eminence. I only met one shady character there, and he was an Englishman. That there are rogues in Melbourne I readily admit. As I was passing up Bourke Street looking for a place to rest in till my friend's carriage, with his lady, was to call for me to take me to his handsome suburban residence, a well-dressed man accosted me with an inquiry as to how I had been enjoying myself since I landed from the *Liguria*. Having replied, I said I was going to have a cup of coffee and a cigar in a handsome *café* just opposite where we were standing. After I had been seated a few minutes he made his appearance to tell me that he was staying at the Melbourne Club, membership of which is the sign and seal of the most extreme respectability; that he was going to England in the *Austral* (I had told him I was going in that ship to Adelaide) in consequence of the delicacy of his wife's health, and that he wished me to come along with him to introduce me to a few friends. I went with him, and in a few minutes was seated in the bar-room of an adjoining hotel, refusing every offer to have a drink. A man came up to my friend with a bill, requesting payment, as he was hard up. Accordingly my gentleman put his hand in his pocket, pulling out three or four sovereigns. Alas! he was a sovereign short. Could I lend him one? Unfortunately I could not. 'Could I lend him half-a-sovereign?' I again deplored my inability to do anything of the kind.

'It does not matter,' he said. Turning to the man he continued, 'Come over the way and I will get the money,' and away he went, telling me he would be back in five minutes. I waited ten, but it is needless to say I saw him no more. Leaving the pub, I met a policeman.

'Have you any rogues about here?' I asked.

'I should say we had,' replied the policeman, with a grin; 'why, last month we had one out here from New York. He said he thought he knew the ropes pretty well, but he felt like a child out here.'

If this policeman's tale be true, Melbourne must indeed be marvellous in more senses than one. To my mind the most marvellous part of Melbourne is to be found in its suburbs. Melbourne is fortunate in this respect. All along the seashore the coast is lined with handsome residences, quite equal in every respect to those of our London merchant princes. At one of them, where I spent a couple of happy days, I found residing in wealth and comfort a son of the well-known and still-lamented, in Nonconformist and Liberal circles, Mr. Grimwade, of Ipswich. He calls his place Harleston, the name of the little sleepy East Anglian town in which he was born. The colonists love the old English names. In the aristocratic quarter known as Toorak I spent a pleasant day with Mr. Murray Smith, the one man whom all the Victorians regard as the most refined of gentlemen, and most able of politicians. In London, as some of my readers may remember, Mr. Murray Smith, as Agent General, was quite as much a social success as he is at home. He calls his place Repton, in memory of his old Derbyshire Grammar School. I discovered the Rev. J. J. Halley, the energetic secretary of the Australian Congregational Union, living in a pretty villa at Camberwell, which he ventures to call Irwell, a stream to most Englishmen who have ever been at Manchester, somewhat dark and malodorous. It is thus the colonists keep up the tender memories of their far-off native land. As in New South Wales, so in Victoria, a good deal of attention is turned to politics. In the latter colony the Parliament lasts three years, and a general election was at hand ; but the worst of it is, that while the people are in many quarters determined to have a fight, in reality there is nothing to fight about. I attended what was advertised as a monster meeting of the Liberal party, but the attendance did not consist of more than 400, and the speaking was, at any rate, not up to the English level, though one speaker did somehow manage to close with an irrelevant peroration, in which he invoked the spirit which in England had carried Catholic emancipation, had removed the Test and Corporation Acts, and was prepared to do justice to Ireland—and this was in connection with a meeting called to support the Liberal platform, the main article of which is protection to native industry and a stock tax for the farmer, who complains bitterly of the way in which New South Wales and Queensland beef is poured into the home market. It seems strange to read of a candidate appealing to the electors for support as 'A Liberal and Protectionist.' But the fact is, in Victoria everyone is a Protectionist, and on the vital issues of the past the community is now at one. A coalition Government is in office, and it is hard to see how any other can exist. A nationalist party is now in course of formation, which has for its object Australian unity, to be accomplished by free inter-colonial interchange. In the meanwhile the Liberals seem to have only to fight about the constitution of the present Government—their chief complaint being that the Liberal element in it is not sufficiently strong.

Zeno tells us that a man has two ears and one mouth, that he may say little and hear much. Australian M.P.'s are quite of a different way of thinking. Of the late Victorian Parliament, a critic in *The Melbourne Argus* writes that during its existence 'the worst elements in the Assembly have had sway instead of the better.' Of all methods of blocking business, none is so plausible as that of moving the adjournment of the House. In nine cases out of ten, a review says, such motions result in a mere waste of time. Another nuisance is the habit of speaking often and long, as every member is entitled to speak once on every question before the House, and as often as he likes when in Committee. This kind of obstruction is raised into an art, and is called 'stonewalling.' As to indecent language, I find one M.P. calling a judge of a neighbouring colony 'a ruffian and a scoundrel, and a bloody-minded man,' referring to the Chief Secretary as being 'as ignorant as a pig on the subject,' and, in short, acting as much like an Irish patriotic M.P. at home as was possible. Again, I found a gentleman who was afflicted with heart disease, and whom nothing but a sense of duty kept at his post, is referred to by an honourable M.P. as follows: 'But nobody takes any notice of a dying man. He is going to be wafted aloft.' Again, a Mr. Jones, referring to a Mr. Reid, said: 'The Hon. Member for Fitzroy with his cavernous mouth could laugh louder than the rest of the Assembly. That cavernous mouth of his was the only thing the hon. member had to connect him with other people. He had a mouth to laugh at a joke, but no brains to originate one.' Again, another M.P. spoke of Sir Graham Berry as 'that miserable old counterfeit, that white-haired political rogue, that bandy-legged old schemer.' After this it is not surprising to read how the same orator, in the course of a scene which occurred on his being called to order, spoke of a fellow M.P. as one who had tried to diddle a barmaid out of threepence! It really seems as if Parliamentary institutions had become effete. In New South Wales the Dibbs Ministry has already been hurled from office. I have seen alike its rise and fall, and it is evident that at Sydney, as in Melbourne, the obstructionists will be strong enough, not to do any good themselves, but to interfere with anyone wishing to achieve any good for the colony whatever.

The Trades Political Platform made its appearance at Melbourne when I was there. It consists of fifteen planks, the chief of which are the maintenance and extension of protection to local industries, the extension of the same principle to the farming and grazing industry by an adequate increase in the duty on imported cereals and stock, the representation of labour on public boards and the commission of the peace, an Eight Hours Legislation Bill (in Victoria the shops are closed at an early hour by Act of Parliament), the abolition of plural voting, the introduction of a Bill to prevent criminal and pauper labour in the community—rather hard this, in a colony where the pauper desires to work, and, able-bodied as many of her paupers are, is really qualified for labour—the extension of the franchise to seamen. Women voters are favoured by the Liberals, though there is a good deal to be said on the other side of the question. As it is, the women do interfere. For instance, amongst the Melbourne candidates is a gentleman who has unfortunately acquired an undesirable reputation. The ladies have met, and resolved that he is not a fit and proper person to represent a respectable constituency. The gentleman in question sneers at the meeting as a hole-and-corner one, but I find several ministers of religion took part in it. Indeed, I think all denominations were represented with the exception of the clergy of the Church of England, who are as little inclined to co-operate with other bodies out here as they are at home. As a further indication of the political opinion forming in the Australian colonies, I note that many of the candidates for Parliamentary election are in favour of a tax on absentees, which, however, is but a small matter after all, as there is a growing tendency on the part of wealthy colonists to remain out here rather than settle in the old country. I question whether in the colonies there is much chance of the 'One man one vote' being carried. It finds no favour in the Second Chamber, to which here, as at home, many sober people look as the bulwark of constitutional freedom. The worst thing I know about Melbourne is its gambling. *The Melbourne Daily Telegraph*, writing of the last grand race—the race which the ladies make the occasion of the display of all that is novel or charming in toilettes, estimates the bets made with the bookmakers between Derby Day and Steeplechase Day as amounting to £700,000, and calculates that 'the stakes, the cost and keep of the horses, the revenues of the *five hundred racing clubs* of the colony, the expenditure of its army of book-makers, and other forms of expenditure,' will bring the racing budget for the year up to £800,000 sterling. We in England are bad enough in this respect I admit, but there is no reason whatever why Australia should follow a bad example.

CHAPTER V.

A LITTLE ABOUT NEW SOUTH WALES.

Sunny Sydney—Public Buildings—Educational Establishments—Sanitary State—Its Climate—Bathurst—The Blue Mountains—Romish Aggression—Botany Bay—Old Days—A Wonderful Change—New South Wales Scenery.

IF you feel disposed to have a look at Sydney, respected reader, do not go there when an election is on. Last night, till eleven, the street in which I have found a temporary residence was filled with an excited crowd, hooting and cheering, as from time to time great placards were posted up as to the result of the day's elections. Wherever I have been, the talk has been of Free Trade or Protection. The farmers want Protection; the towns are averse to it. High railway charges deprive the farmer of his Sydney market, and he is undersold by the foreigner. The Free Traders are obliged to hedge to satisfy the workman. He can't stand the Chinese, and more than one Free Trade candidate has had to promise to vote for prohibitory duties on articles of Chinese manufacture. Another one declared that he was against Protection, but would be quite ready to tax foreign goods for fiscal purposes—that is, for protection for the New South Wales manufacturer. The Free Traders have won, but they will go to Parliament with diminished force. There is a good deal of nonsense talked here as well as in England. One M.P. complained recently 'about the absence of his name *appearing* in the Sydney morning papers.' Said another, as he banged the balcony bar with his fist, 'Don't you think, gentlemen, that there was some grave *misapprehension* of the public money during the time that the Parkes party was in power.' Another had the hardihood to venture on the use of a French term, as he dilated on what he called 'the scandalis doin's of the Parkes *rejamey*.' But a certain candidate who shall be nameless heads the list (or, as they say out here, the 'bunch') of blundering orators when he remarked that 'If the days of miracles were as common as in the days of Ananias, they might expect to see three of the finest pillars of salt that ever were on view.' One lesson we may learn—that is, the advantage of having the elections all over on the same day, and that is how it is done in Victoria. Here the struggle continues for three weeks, and a good deal of bad feeling is engendered in consequence.

In spite of the dust and the heat—to change my theme—there is much to admire in Sydney, and I have had a fine look at the town from the lofty tower of the new Post Office, a tower some 260 feet above the level of George Street, where it stands. Afar off are the Heads, into which the great steamers come and go. At your feet lies the city, with its fine public buildings, all of yellow sandstone; its narrow streets, its busy crowds. Far as the eye can reach in every direction spread pretty suburbs, and there the foliage begins to mingle with the gray roofs and white chimneys of the suburban houses, and you realize the fact how great is the population outside the city itself. The harbour is a thing of beauty and a joy for ever; how Cook could have missed it seems a mystery. Over that harbour the fine river steamers—of American fashion, far superior to anything we have on the Thames —ferry backwards and forwards all day long. On a Saturday it is alive with yachts—little cockle-shells, with two great sails, that soon upset. I saw one capsize in a sudden squall as I was crossing to Manly Beach—the Brighton of Sydney, as they call it here, but it is no more like our Brighton than a rustic maiden resembles a society beauty. All along the harbour are fairy villas, green foliage, miniature bays, rivers, and all that can give life and warmth to the landscape in the shape of holiday-makers. That harbour, with its Botanical Gardens on one side, alone would compensate for a good deal, and reconcile one even to the crowds of Sydney who fill up the streets at night and prevent all enjoyment. Sunday is quite a relief. It is a day of rest indeed, far more so than in England. In the morning, instead of going to the noble cathedral, I turned into the Congregational Church in Pitt Street, but the minister was away, and so I fancy were his people, as the place was but half full; but I am told on a Sunday night there is a very fine congregation. Four or five hundred young men were met in the fine building known as the Y.M.C.A., where they listened with much interest to the address delivered by the Secretary, Mr. Walker, and at a temperance hall near there was a service fairly attended; while close by, the New Church were meeting for public worship. In the evening there was a good deal of open-air preaching. In one quarter I heard so much from a young man about the ''oly hangels' that I was compelled to retreat. Christian effort is not out of place anywhere in Australia, and apparently in Sydney least of all. The churches have quite as much to contend against there as at home.

A Little About New South Wales.

Crime and pauperism and vice, strange as it may seem, are quite as plentiful in this land of gold and milk and honey as at home. Alas! you may change the climate, but the man remains the same.

One of the blots of Sydney is the street tramcar, drawn by a snorting engine, which makes night and day hideous. As a nuisance and a means of getting rid of the surplus population it seems an admirable contrivance. The cabs are not bad, and the drivers quite as civil as those at home, which, however, is not saying much; but the omnibuses are very old and shaky, and at times the noise they make is so great that conversation is quite out of the question. The Chinese are everywhere, and when they are driven away it is hard to see how the townspeople will get their fruit or their vegetables—as the Anglo-Saxons, whether native or Australian, seem to hold gardening in contempt, whereas the heathen Chinee will get hold of a bit of waste land which no one would ever think of tilling, and straightway it rejoices and blossoms as the rose. Many of them are tradesmen, and have shops in the best streets in the place. For cabinet-making of all kinds they have quite a talent, but they have few friends, although, as a tradesman in Sydney remarked to me, 'They are a good deal better than the people who find fault with them.'

Sydney, like Melbourne and Adelaide, rejoices in a university based on the model of University College, London, and established by the State in 1850. Its buildings are magnificent, and a portion of them are set apart for the School of Medicine attached. The prospects of the university are excellent, and it cannot fail to exert a most beneficial influence on the future of Australia. The Australian Museum, which is the oldest institution of the kind in Australia, occupies a conspicuous site in Sydney, facing one of the principal parks; it is open on Sundays. One of the most popular institutions of the town is the Free Public Library, which, in 1877, had a lending branch attached to it to meet the wants of country residents. The National Art Gallery, established in 1880, is also open on Sundays. It contains an excellent collection of paintings and statuary, comprising some of the most famous works of the best modern artists of the old world, and includes several very valuable gifts from private persons. The extent of streets and lanes within the boundaries of the city is 105 miles, and they are mostly in good order, many of them being laid with wood blocks. Its new Town Hall, opened since I left, is the finest on the continent. The great difficulty in Sydney, and all over New South Wales, seems to be house accommodation. The poor have a hard time of it as regards sleeping apartments, and one does not envy the occupiers of the little corrugated iron-roofed shanties in which, as a rule, the workman hides his diminished head. In all our great towns the artisans have better homes than they have in Sydney and the other Australian towns. Then there is the drought to make everything in the shape of agricultural produce or garden stuff dear, with the exception of meat, which is about half the price that it is at home. Eggs are scarce, milk is fourpence a quart, and, as far as I can learn, other provisions are very little cheaper than in London. In sanitary arrangements the colonies are far behind the old country. In his retiring address, the President of the Victorian Branch of the Medical Association, Dr. Rowan, denounces the 'infamous' acts committed by land syndicates, who, in laying out their townships, acted as if they considered drainage a prejudice, sunlight a delusion, and ventilation a weakness to be treated with derision. If ever, said he, a city rendered itself liable to be plague-stricken, it was Melbourne. I don't know whether a similar remark applies to Sydney, but I do know that there the rate of infant mortality is alarmingly high. In Australia, as in the old country, they have not yet learned what to do with their sewage. In Sydney they laid out a million of money, and then discovered that they had simply poured all their filth into the harbour; but Sydney has now seen the error of its ways, and at enormous expense constructed a tunnel many miles long to take the sewage right away to the sea. At Melbourne the smell from the Yarra river is overpowering. In Adelaide they have solved the difficulty, and have a sewage farm that pays well; but Adelaide is a small place when compared with Sydney or Melbourne. A good deal remains to be done if the health of the great colonial towns is to be preserved. Equally important is the water question. What is wanted are tanks that shall conserve the rainwater when it falls. I have ridden miles and miles and seen great rivers nothing but beds of sand, and creeks, where the winter torrents flow, nothing but great fissures in the parched plains, in which the cattle hide themselves from the blazing sun. New South Wales can never prosper till it has a proper water supply. To provide this should be the first duty of the Government. I suppose it is because people make their money quickly that the Government grant so many holidays. It is a great nuisance this to merchants and traders. You rush off to the bank, and find it shut up, and on the door a notice to the effect

A Little About New South Wales. 117

that it is Bank-holiday. The mass of the people work on all the same. A Bank-holiday in no way concerns them, and consequently a Bank-holiday here has little likeness to the similar function at home—when all our big cities empty their living crowds to be a wonder and a terror to all the country round. The public offices are always being closed on some pretence or another. Sometimes it is an agricultural show, sometimes it is a race ; any excuse does. And the bankers' clerks, as regards hours, are much better off than their brethren at home ; in all parts of Australia the banks are closed at three.

It is a fair land, this new Australian continent, and well worthy to be inhabited by the energetic Anglo-Saxon race. The whole mountain system of New South Wales lies below the limit of perpetual snow. The grandeur of the scenery is not to be compared with that of the Alps or the Rocky Mountains. On the contrary, from the plains, the mountains look rather insignificant ; but once on them, and looking into the gorges below, clothed with verdure, or on the broad plains far beyond, you are struck with the magnificent scale on which Nature has worked in these solitudes. Over all is a mantle of blue haze, which makes the whole effect most striking, and has given to the range of hills visible from Sydney the appropriate name of the Blue Mountains. However, there is nothing equalling the view you get as you enter Sydney through Port Jackson. It is needless to say a word of Sydney harbour. It holds the first place amongst the harbours of the world for convenience of entrance, depth of water, and natural shipping facilities. The area of water surface of the harbour proper is 15 square miles, and the shore line is reckoned to extend 165 miles. Along it are the homes of many of the well-to-do of Sydney, which is the metropolis of New South Wales, and the mother city of the Australians. The city and its suburbs occupy 100 square miles, and accommodate about 350,000 people. I am agreeably disappointed with Sydney. Its shops and public buildings and hotels are handsomer, and its streets broader, than I had anticipated. I was frightened, I own, by what Mr. Froude has written about its mosquitoes. Perhaps mosquitoes do not like me; I am not sorry. Coming to Sydney by sea you feel, on the whole, that Eden cannot be far off.

Nor is the climate so bad as some people fancy. In Naples, where so many English go, the summer is warmer and the winter much colder than at Sydney. The famed resorts on the Mediterranean seaboard, it is now confessed, bear no comparison with the

A Little About New South Wales.

Pacific slope of New South Wales, either for natural salubrity or the comparative mildness of the summer and winter; while the epidemics and pestilences which have devastated the regions of ancient civilization have never made their appearance on Australian shores. The Hawkesbury formation over which the city of Sydney is built provides it with an inexhaustive supply of sandstone of the highest quality for building purposes. The beauty of Sydney street architecture owes much to it, as it is a material admirably adapted for architectural effect, being of a pleasant colour, fine grain, and easily worked.

Sydney is not only the metropolis, but the chief shipping port of the colony, its trade being larger than that of any city in the southern hemisphere. All the necessary tools and appliances for the repairing of ships are found in dockyards. The new graving dock, now being completed by the Government, will be the largest single dock in the world, and capable of receiving vessels drawing 32 feet of water. For natural facilities for shipping Sydney stands unrivalled. The water deepens abruptly from the shores, so that the largest vessels may be berthed alongside the wharves and quays. The Sydneyites love their harbour, and well may they do so, for none fairer is to be found under the sun. 'What do you think of our **harbour?'** is the first question asked a **stranger.** A tale is told of the captain of an English man-of-war which was at anchor here, that he was so tired of the question being constantly put that he had a blackboard hung over the side of his ship, on which he had chalked up, with a view to save trouble and prevent further inquiries: 'We admire your harbour very much.'

It is a curious fact how little the cry of the 'three acres and a cow' seems to affect the people. They will flock to large towns. In England they all go to London. It is the same in America. Land is to be had in abundance, but, nevertheless, the town offers greater inducements than the country. In New South Wales, as in Victoria, this is everywhere the case. The increase of the population of Sydney during the seventeen years which closed with 1887 has been 67 per cent., and that of the suburbs 280 per cent., while that of the country districts amounted to 90 per cent. As usual in a dense city crowd, there are a good many black sheep. A leading police official stated recently that he believed fully 70 per cent. of the inhabitants of the city were directly or indirectly affected by the gambling clubs that obtained amongst them. Public-houses, tobacconists' shops, and clubs were in a vast number of cases but gambling houses in disguise. In Sydney there is consequently a good deal of poverty, and last winter relief works were established for the benefit of some three thousand unemployed ; yet the skilled artisan gets good wages, and as I write the plasterers are out on strike for an advance of 1s. per day as wages, the present rate being 10s.—not bad when one remembers Sydney enjoys free-trade prices, and that there is no protracted winter to interfere with building operations. These unemployed had as rations ten pounds of flour, ten pounds of meat, two pounds of sugar and a quarter of a pound of tea, with a minimum wage of 3s. per day, and that day, it must be remembered, is but eight hours' work. The result of this kindness was that Sydney, as long as the work lasted, was filled with idle loafers and vagabonds from all the country round. Charity seems to do a deal of mischief abroad as well as at home.

Of the original inhabitants of the country you see few traces, either in New South Wales or in Victoria. It is in Queensland and South Australia that they most abound. They have been badly treated by the whites, and in many cases they took a horrible revenge. They now give little trouble, and work peacefully for their former enemies. Amongst their good qualities are a love of religious mystery, a stoical contempt for pain, and a deep reverence for their departed friends and ancestors. The only unpleasant characteristic of the present inhabitants of New South Wales is the broad line of demarcation between Churchmen and Dissenters. Often the Church of England man in the colonies looks upon all Dissenters with aversion. The other day I heard of a little girl who was forbidden to play with the intelligent and pretty daughter of a wealthy colonist on the plea that she was a Dissenter, and consequently not a fitting associate for the daughter of a Church of England lady. Let me give another illustration. I have just heard of a clergyman who told a mother that it would be better to have her child baptized by a Roman priest than by a Dissenting minister!

I am staying in a gentleman's house. No sooner had the *Orizaba* dropped anchor than it was boarded by a gentleman, who kindly took me off, and away to the railway station, and personally conducted me over the Blue Mountains by the celebrated Zigzag Railway, which deserves all that can be said in its favour. It is a wonderful achievement in the way of engineering, as it climbs the Blue Mountains, that favourite health resort of Sydney, on one side, and descends on the other. In one place you catch sight of the track three times; you see the line you have left, you see that on which you travel, and you see, lower down, that on which, in another moment, you will be travelling. It is wonderful, but not quite up to the trip over the Alleghanies, and I enjoyed it, though the heat was great, and the rocks and valleys seemed as much burnt up as those of Aden itself.

In due time we reached Bathurst, where I was met by a joyous party of youngsters, who bundled me into a carriage drawn by a couple of handsome horses, and in a little while I found myself seated in the charming country residence of the Hon. E. Webb, a member of the Upper House, who came from Saltash, and who has certainly gained here both fame and fortune. Bathurst, I take it, may be considered a fair specimen of an Australian county town, and the Bathurst people are certainly more devoted to its welfare than are people at home to that of the localities in which they reside. The place is laid out with an eye to the future, and the streets are a great deal broader than our Portland Place. The houses and shops are rather mixed, some of them being built of brick, lofty and commodious, while others are wooden shanties which would not be tolerated at home. The public buildings are fine. The town is governed by a mayor and corporation. It has a very handsome court-house, a magnificent hospital, which is not in debt, and has—how unlike our English ones!—£3,000 to its credit in the treasurer's hands. Its churches of all kinds are good; and even the little churches in which the Baptists and Independents meet are clean and comfortable. Out here one would have thought the Baptists and Independents might have worshipped together; but no, they must meet in separate bodies, as at home. The Presbyterians have a fine church, which must have cost a good deal of money, but when I looked in on Sunday evening the worshippers were a mere handful. Surely some of these churches might unite, and be all the stronger for so doing.

The only drawback here is the heat, which does terrible mischief. We are 2,000 feet above the level of the sea, and the people call it cool because the thermometer is something under a hundred in the shade. The clouds come up, but they bring no rain. At night we have a cool breeze, but, unfortunately, just as one feels comfortable, and that life is worth living, everyone goes to bed. Soon after my arrival I had a country drive. There had been a bush fire, and my host sent me and one of his nephews to see what amount of mischief had been done. Away we dashed merrily, drawn by a pair of young horses that scarcely turned a hair, along the sandy road, over the rolling downs. Leaving Bathurst behind, we were soon in what in England we should call a waste, howling wilderness, and yet a few days of rain would make all that plain a monster park, where the sheep could graze, and everyone would rejoice. For miles we saw no living thing, and no sign of civilization save the fences—of rails, very high, as the cattle have a bad habit of jumping them. We met a young lady riding into Bathurst, holding the horse's reins in one hand and her parasol in the other, a waggon drawn by ten oxen coming into the town with wood, and a cart or two—that was all. We passed over a fine bridge, but the bed of the river was dry. Far ahead of us was a cloud of smoke from a bush-fire, a calamity of constant occurrence in such warm weather. Soon we were in a forest ourselves, ghastly with the withered grass and the stumps of old trees not yet decayed, with the white trunks and grotesque branches twisted in all directions, but leafless, and gum-trees that are ring-barked—the common mode of destroying trees in this part of the country. Now and then I saw an unfortunate cow, vainly seeking green grass, or cool water, or the grateful shade, and half-starved all the while; or a hare, as big again as that of England, and breeding much more rapidly in this precocious clime. Presently a couple of magpies passed us, and they are much larger than at home. But life of any kind is rare, and we got on to the hillside where the fire had been, and saw everything black and charred, trees fallen down, fences only a black line of charcoal. One could fancy that everything living had fallen a prey to the devouring flame. Up in the bush, on a hill on our left, there were kangaroos, but they unfortunately did not put in an appearance; and if I saw three emus in the course of my ride, candour compels me to own that they were tame, in a gentleman's grounds, and not in their native state. The great pests of this part of the world are the flies. I don't mind them on the table, if they do make the white sugar apparently a heap of black, or if they do darken the snow-white tablecloth; it is only when they proceed to attack the company around that I think they carry their jokes too far. They are a special torment to the baldheaded, but they disdain not the fairest of the fair. The New South Wales flies are smaller than those of the mother country, and twice as mischievous. To them there is nothing sacred; and as to the forty winks grateful to many of us after luncheon or dinner, they are quite out of the question.

The English fruit-grower complains of the wet and cold, the Australian of the heat and drought. The

Ex-Mayor of Sydney tells me he has lost £10,000 worth of sheep this season in consequence of the heat; and the charming daughter of my host, who resides with her husband at a station a hundred and fifty miles further north—and in Australia the further you go north the hotter it becomes—has been driven away from her husband, and has to come here with her children because they have no water nearer than eight miles. As I write I see the signs of a water famine everywhere, in the dusty road, in the parched fields, in the distant hills far away. The only exception is the garden, consisting of many acres beautifully laid out and well shaded with trees of all kinds. Mr. Webb, my host, has a tank which conveys the water everywhere, and even the lawn-tennis ground beyond, to which the young men and maidens seem as devoted as they are at home, abounds with verdure. The mansion, for such it is, rises out of a garden of roses and dahlias, and luxurious flowers, blooming and bright to look on; while behind are apple and plum and pear and greengage and mulberry trees laden with luscious fruit to any amount. Some of the flowers, the stocks, for instance, take far brighter colours than they do at home; the greengages, too, are finer than ours, owing to the same reason—the abundance of sun, a sun which makes the Australian hornet, with its blue gauze wings, as black as a coal-heaver.

As to the servants in this house, I dare not say what wages they are getting. All I know is, that if I were a lady-help, or even a servant of all-work, it would not be long ere I booked my passage for New South Wales. The coachman has a hundred a year and his house, and the gardener not much less. It is needless to add that I find it good to be here : it is hard that I must take up my bed and walk. Here no iron horse screams as he urges on his wild career, no noisy screw perpetually churns up the troubled sea ; I hear no hoarse watchman, as the hour strikes, proclaiming in the midnight air, 'All's well ': here no newsboy makes the land hideous with his noise, nor does the gin-drinking tramp interfere with my peaceful digestion. Most weary seems the sea—

> ' Weary the oar,
> Weary the wandering fields of foam.'

Yes, like the mild-eyed, melancholy Lotos Eaters, I feel it is sweet to sit me down upon the yellow sand and

> ' Dream of Fatherland,
> Of child, and wife, and slave.'

But I am back in Sydney, and seek to study its ways. We hold the Church of Rome, in all ages and in all countries, to be the foe of freedom, civil and religious, the great obstacle in the way of progress, and the worst enemy of God and man; it is but natural that its growth in New South Wales and all Australia gives one alarm. It fights with an immense advantage over its opponents by reason of its wealth, its effective organization, and its Irish allies, who are banded together for its support in every colony, and, I may add, in every land. The only priest I have as yet met with was a model of good-temper and good-humour, and had an enormous advantage in every way over his ritualistic ally, who does his work unconsciously, and burns his fingers by pulling the chestnuts out of the fire for him. In New South Wales it is understood that the Romanists are discontented with the existing Education Act, which is undenominational, and they have supported the Protectionists, not out of love for them, but with the hope to get some of the public money for their schools, or, at any rate, modifications in the school system which may be favourable to themselves. As it is, they do not fare badly. The other day it was discovered that a school teacher had, in spite of his duty to be neutral, gone out of his way to teach Romanist doctrines to his pupils. A fuss was made about it, but he was only removed to another school, that was all. Again, at a place called Waratah, it has been decided that there shall be no intramural burials. The principal of the monastery there writes to the Municipal Council for the privilege to bury members of the monastery in their own grounds. The Council are divided, and the Mayor gives the casting vote in favour of the monastery, that is, in favour of breaking the laws of his borough. Now, it is very evident that if any Protestant parson, any Baptist or Wesleyan or Presbyterian, had pleaded for anything of the kind, that is, for power to break the sanitary laws of the borough, and to have a private burying-ground of their own, they would have pleaded in vain. In Victoria, four or five years ago, there was such an uprising that there has since been no Catholic party in the House of any size whatever. It is well to note here that in the eyes of the State, all over Australia, religions are on an equality. Under Sir Richard Bourke all religions received State aid; but in 1862 this was put a stop to, and all that the State now does is to pension off the survivors under the old *régime*. In this way last year, in New South Wales, was divided between the Church of England, the Roman Catholic Church, the Presbyterians and the Methodists, about £10,000, the Church of England, as was to be expected, taking the lion's share. When the sparseness of the population is considered, the church attendance will appear very large; and, though apparently less than found in the colony of Victoria, it is, proportionately, much larger than in England. In the Bush, the Church of England parsons seem to be somewhat remiss in the performance of their duties. A lady residing in the interior tells me that she went to the Church of England preaching station frequently, but the parson never turned up, and she had to return unblessed.

Yesterday I took the tramcar—a Government institution, by-the-bye—and had a look at Botany Bay, a place of many evil memories, and whose associations reach very far, even now that it has no terrors for the criminal or reprobate. In reality, Botany Bay was not the penal settlement; that was at Sydney; but the popular mind believed all the convicts were sent to Botany Bay, and hence my use of the term. In a recently published correspondence, a distinguished Victorian judge asserts: 'An uneasy and uninformed feeling of suspicious dislike of England and her Government, which is not without a justifying cause, undoubtedly exists, and is growing, in these communities. Its extent is not ascertainable, but it may safely be affirmed that it will depend largely upon the relations which yet remain to be acknowledged and to be established between the Imperial and Colonial Governments of her Majesty in the immediate future, whether this feeling will not soon expand among native Australians into one of profound and general alienation.' I think the judge is right, and that this feeling is growing stronger, finding expression, not in the old-established papers of the colony, such as *The Melbourne Argus* or *The Sydney Morning Herald,* papers of great wealth and influence, but among their younger and less fortunate rivals. 'It was England,' writes one of them, 'that first seamed the white shoulder of Australia with the livid mark of the lash. It is the people who wielded that instrument of degradation, and their descendants, who wish to draw the bonds of Empire closer to-day. The Imperial connection is, therefore, a shameful one.' Poor Captain Cook had a good deal to answer for when, in an evil moment, he first dropped his anchor in Botany Bay. It was quite a mistake to send out our criminals there; they should have been allowed, says young Australia, to die of gaol-fever at home. But, says young Australia, England in her wickedness did more—it colonized a continent where the English spirit of the time was to be perpetuated by the transmitted influence of the gaolers of these convicts long after a new Liberalism had entered into British politics, and long after the

A Little About New South Wales. 133

narrow spirit of a hundred years ago, with convictism itself, had passed away. The contention of a growing class in Australia is that the enduring effect of the convict system on the public spirit of the older Australian colonies is traceable, not so much to the convicts themselves, as to their gaolers. These are the mercenary wretches to be gibbeted for the scorn of every honest man. These are the gods whom the Australians ignorantly worship, whose spirit is still strong to deprive the horny-handed of his rights; who were the founders of the vile system which actually gives property an influence in making laws, and in determining the political character of the country; men who made colossal fortunes by the illegitimate sale of rum. The chief constable of Sydney had actually a license to sell rum; and, as Dr. Laing puts it, 'the chief gaoler, though not exactly permitted to convert the gaol into a grog shop, had a licensed house in which he sold rum publicly on his own behalf right opposite the gaol door.' The convicts, it is admitted, for the sake of argument, were some of them bad; but as to their gaolers—the gallant men of the New South Wales Corps, for instance—they were all rascals; and they were the founders of Australia, and their spirit lives and dominates in the political institutions of the country to this day. It seems to me that this is a foul libel on the country, though it is the indictment put forth by an Australian writer in an Australian newspaper. Australians are not much given to the study of history, and perhaps it is well. History is of little avail when it is treated in this way. Australia was not all Botany Bay, and its leaders are men whose fathers, by their character and enterprise and industry, distinguished themselves in the fair land to which they had come penetrated with English ideas, with English habits, with the English Bible, with Milton, and Shakespeare, and Burns; and it is to them, rather than to Botany Bay, that Australia owes its greatness and its power, its present flourishing state, its capabilities—when its mines are developed, when its vast continent has been opened up by settlement, and a general system of irrigation —of a greater future. It is true, I read in some of the weekly papers, that Australia is tyrannized over by wealthy imbeciles, while the high-souled horny-handed is left out in the cold; that the present state of things is infamous, and must be put an end to. So far as I can see, the horny-handed is master of the situation. I admit that he is not a bad fellow. I wish that he were a little more civil, a little more patriotic, and that his women-folk were not so egregiously over-dressed. For his own sake, also, I own that I wish his better-half knew how to cook a steak and boil a potato. What I maintain—and what his admirers will not admit—is that the capitalist, the successful working-man, who has improved himself out of his original poverty, who has acquired wealth, and all the good it brings with it, is at any rate his equal. To talk of the taint of Botany Bay is the silliest of bunkum in the world. There is no trace of it now. Young Australia knows nothing of transportation. In Australia you face a new world, a world as new to the writers filled with tales of the horrors of transportation and gaoler officialism, and the cringing subservience which it engendered, as was Botany Bay to Captain Cook, whose monument I see placed in the park opposite the Sydney Museum. It could not but be so, when the gold discoveries overran the country with a population at the rate of 90,000 arrivals in a year—a mixed population if you like, but mostly free, and many of them as manly a set of fellows as any to be met with anywhere. It is an ill bird that defiles its own nest, and the Australian who endeavours to make political capital by dwelling on the blunders of the old country in its efforts to colonize, and thereby creates an antagonistic feeling to England, does injustice alike to his own colony and the Fatherland.

But, after all, I have said little of Botany Bay itself, which remains much the same in its natural features as when Cook landed there a century ago. The tramway plants you on the shore—all white sand and dead seaweed. Afar you see the narrow entrance into the Pacific, along which Cook cautiously steered his ship, and opposite, on the wooded shore on the other side, is a small black monument to denote where the great circumnavigator landed. It is a peaceful spot: woods are all round, the jerry-builder has neglected the spot altogether, and the Sydneyite comes here, with his wife and family, for an occasional mouthful of sea air. On one side of you is a pier, and in another spot I see an intimation that boats are to be had for hire, but no boat disturbs the tranquil bay as I wander alone by the sad sea-shore. To me, meditating, there comes a vision of the old world, when George III. was living. I see the black man watching sullenly the new arrivals, frightened by neither their appearance nor their bullets—which they fire just to awaken the native, who returns a shower of arrows. It is curious how the black has disappeared, how firmly the white man has planted himself in his seat, and with what bitterness he has come to regard as an interloper the heathen Chinee—who seems to muster pretty strongly in the busy, half-built territory that stretches from the bay to the capital. As I get into the train I am sandwiched between two celestials, so I dream visions. Is the world for the future to be given up to the Mongolian? Is the Caucasian played out? Not exactly, I fancy; at any rate, as far as Australia is concerned.

In South Wales nothing is more remarkable than the elevation—social, political, and religious—of the people, within little more than a single generation. In 1845 Dr. Darwin published his last edition of 'The Voyage of the *Beagle*.' In the course of his voyage he landed at Sydney, and writes: 'On the whole, from what I have heard more than from what I saw, I was disappointed with the state of society. The whole community is rancorously divided into parties on almost every subject. Among those who from their station in life ought to be the best, many live in such open profligacy that respectable people cannot live with them. There is much jealousy between the children of the rich emancipist and the free settlers, the former being pleased to consider honest men as interlopers.' Darwin also refers to the mischief done to the children by the degraded class of servants by whom they are surrounded. In the New South Wales of to-day, not only do you see nothing of this, but quite the reverse. It forms the grandest illustration the world has yet seen of the tendency of human society to elevate and reform itself.

I would also say something of the country. New South Wales is not dependent solely on its harbour nor its Blue Mountains for beauty. I heard everywhere much of the beauty of the Hunter River district, and the richness of its soil, but I regret I was unable to visit it. I did go, however, to the Hawkesbury River, not a long ride by rail from Sydney—the Rhine of New South Wales, as Mr. Trollope terms it. It is not the Rhine, no more than is the Hudson River of New York. Both are charming rivers for a day's outing, but they are not the Rhine with its old castles, its vine-clad hills, its legendary lore. There is but one Rhine in the world, as there is but one Thames. However, on the Hawkesbury you have lovely scenery, tranquil waters, wooded hills, a beauteous solitude, an air of repose, which make one realize how divine is Nature and all her works. It was good to be there. It was with regret that I tore myself away.

CHAPTER VI.

AMONGST THE BANANA BOYS.

Collision in Sydney Harbour—Brisbane—The Banana Boys—
Sir Samuel Griffith.

'IT is too hot for any Englishman to go to Sydney in January and February,' said a gentleman to me on board the *Orizaba*—but I went. At Sydney every- one said it was too hot to think of going to Brisbane —but I went; and in either case I should have missed a great deal of pleasure had I stayed away. The misfortune was that I went by the *Warrago* to Brisbane, a favourite boat, and the crowd was so great I had to sleep in the dining-saloon; but the trip was enjoyable. In the first place, to start with, we had a real collision at sea, and I had time to calculate what my chances were of ever seeing my native land again as I watched with not a little interest the attacking vessel steering steadily for our steamer's side. Fortunately she got the worst of it, as her foresail and bowsprit came tumbling down, and we made our way out in safety. I don't think anyone was to blame. The fact was, just as we were starting a Melbourne ship, the *Barcoo*, was leaving the wharf. Between us was an unhappy schooner laden with coal, and her choice lay simply between Scylla and Charybdis. The former she cleared; the latter she ran into. Methinks I heard her infuriated captain, as he looked athwart his damaged barque, scream out something disrespectful concerning land-lubbers. Our gallant captain, however, in a conversation with me on the subject, explained that the other party was entirely in the wrong. Be that as it may, it seemed to me rather hard that the only occasion on which, as he told me, he ever met with an accident should have been when I was on board.

Our trip was vastly agreeable, as we saw a good deal of the Australian coast under very favourable circumstances, the sea being calm and the skies bright. In about thirty-six hours we had reached the mouth of Moreton Bay, a fine sheet of water, with the conical hills on our right which Cook called 'the Glass Houses,' and then by a narrow channel we made our way into the river on which Brisbane stands, and which bears its name. When the tide is up the Brisbane river is almost as romantic as our lovely Dart, and a good deal more so than our far-famed Orwell. Only think of mangroves growing right up from the water for miles, of banks where the bananas ripen, and where you can pluck juicy mangoes from the stalk (on the top of the banks I saw the graceful bamboo), where strange flowers bloomed and strange birds shrieked (the native Australian bird never sings), where the pineapple (they were selling them at Brisbane at a penny each) grows in the open, and where actually I saw for the first time the sugar-cane reared in the field, and felt as Alice must have felt in Wonderland.

Queensland, the youngest, promises to be the most flourishing of the colonies. It was not till 1859 that it was known to the world as Queensland; up to that time it had formed a portion of New South Wales. Queensland is still open to emigrants, and its Government lends a helping hand, unlike the other colonies, to emigrants of the right sort. On the Darling plains they can live in comfort, but, alas! they cannot all expect to settle there. It is in the north that the most astonishing progress has been within the last quarter of a century, and alas! the north is hot— hotter than the average Englishman can stand. Mining and sugar-growing are the leading industries of the north. In many instances the former has proved the primary factor in the opening of new territory, and in the extension of trade to ports in the higher latitudes. Notable instances of this may be seen to-day in the townships of Cooktown and Cairns, which owe their origin entirely to the goldfields of the Palmer and Hodgkinson. In the case of the latter, the discovery of the extremely fruitful nature of the soil has induced settlement, and agriculture is looked upon as one of the principal means of ensuring a thriving future. Brisbane is not as remarkable as either Melbourne or Sydney. To begin with, it has only a population of some 74,000, though it is the capital of 668,224 square miles. They can grow everything, apparently, and find everything, for its mineral treasures are beyond conception. It is Queensland that owns the great Morgan Mine which just now has turned everybody's head; but in no part of Australia have I seen so much that tells of growth and progress. All over the place they are pulling down the old shanties and erecting fine buildings in their stead, of stone white as marble. Outside, the suburbs are pretty, and land is cheap at £1,500 an acre. The Houses of Parliament are stately. The Governor has a handsome residence, and the public gardens are extensive and form an agreeable promenade, before the too hot sun rises, along the river's bank. Afar, forming a landmark, as it were, is an enormous white building, known as All Hallows Convent. I was more interested in the Reformatory, on our left, where, unlike our own, the lads are reformed, not returned to society harder and wickeder than ever. The streets are fairly wide, and some of the shops are handsome. It is a busy place. The town is full of hotels, and, led by the lust of gold, people ever come and go.

'We are Banana boys,' said a young Queenslander to me as we steamed up the river, looking over at the muddy sediment they call whales' spawn. 'We have some smart men among us. Look,' said he, 'there is one,' as he pointed to a tall, light-haired gentleman in gray clothes and soft felt hat—something of the figure of Sir Fowell Buxton. Happily I had no need to have pointed out to me Sir Samuel Griffith, late Premier of Queensland and the head of its Bar. I had introduced myself to him soon after we left Sydney, and never did I meet with a more friendly acquaintance. Naturally, at first he seemed, as he viewed me through his eyeglass, a little suspicious, as are most Colonials, and as they are bound to be when you remember the tales they have to hear, and the doubtful characters who force themselves on their notice. But as we chatted away his reserve relaxed, and he became the charming companion, ready to describe all the country round, and to show me all the kindness in his power. As we stood on the deck he pointed to a handsome white brick-built bungalow rising out of a fine extent of lawn and garden, overlooking the river, with which it was connected. 'That is my house,' said he, at the same time inviting me to dine there that night—an offer which, it is needless to say, I gladly accepted. In due time I reached Merthyr, as Sir Samuel names his residence, from the place in old Wales where he was born, and where, on his recent visit home, he was received with a cordiality such as gallant little Wales only extends once in a way to her most distinguished sons. He, the poor Dissenting minister's son, then the Premier of Queensland, and still the greatest man in the colony—for I never knew a fallen statesman so beloved—was the guest at Cyfartha Castle. I know not why he has gone out of office, but I think the cause is not far to seek. Queensland is split up into two separate camps—the North, who want coloured labour to work on the sugar plantations, a work for which no white man is fit; and the South, who say the black labour of the North is really slavery, and who object to it in every form. To the pretensions of the North Sir Samuel has ever been sternly opposed; and then he had held office five years—and democracies are always fickle. So Sir Samuel is now the leader of Her Majesty's Opposition, and is as much respected and as strong almost as ever. There is an air of refinement about him which tells even with the Banana boys, who look as brown and burnt up as it is possible for men to be. They seem determined men, with felt hats of every shape and colour, with hands that seem never to have known the mysteries of soap and water—men who have done yeomen's work at the diggings, or on the sheep farm — and give you a shake which reminds one strongly of the 'horny-handed.' Ah, they told me some strange tales of the blacks in the little smoke-room of the steamer by which we returned, and would have told me more had it not come on to blow so hard that we were all compelled to go to bed. They all rejected Sir Samuel's policy, as an injury to the North, but they all loved the man, of whom we shall, I doubt not, soon hear again. He is young, as men go—almost too young, you would think, for the power he has grasped. I do not blame him that he resolved to fight out his battle in Queensland rather than return to England to take Henry Richard's place as M.P. for Merthyr, as he was invited to do.

In this respect the father resembles the son. Brisbane is his home. He has reached the term of three score years and ten, and he now holds the pulpit of the Congregationalist chapel at Brisbane till the people have appointed his successor. The day before I reached Brisbane there had been a meeting of his friends to do him honour, and the old man was well pleased at it, as I found from a short talk with him in his pleasant home, not far from his son's ampler residence. The ex-Premier is not a man to be idle. He has faced the problem of the day—the perpetual struggle between want and wealth—and has something to say on the matter. Hardly a care seemed to cloud his brow, hardly a wish to be left unsatisfied. He seemed to me alike sound in head and heart, as we sat smoking under the veranda of his handsome bungalow, under the Southern Cross, with the river running at our feet, with the cry of want and woe silent, with the sound of the distant city hushed, while the moonlight, stealing over the scene, had blended with the lights of eve.

CHAPTER VII.

SOUTH AUSTRALIA.

Holy Adelaide — Its Situation — Its Public Buildings — Its Mining-market—Dr. Arnold—Australian Plagues: Fleas and Mosquitoes and Serpents—Sunday Observance—The Macleay Mission—Number of Churches.

WHY Adelaide, from which I now write, can claim to be called 'the Holy,' is one of these things no 'fellah' can understand. It may be because it is near Paradise, to which, I see, there is a daily service of trains, but which I have not yet visited, partly because I have a conviction that it is a place for which I am not yet ripe, and partly because at present my time is better occupied. Through the kindness of Chief Justice Way, the Acting-Governor of South Australia *pro tem.*, I am an honorary member of the Adelaide Club, and what with the English magazines and newspapers—long denied me —and the members of the club to talk to, I am perfectly contented to forego the joys of Paradise awhile. Chief Justice Way deserves a chapter to himself as the Mecænas of South Australia—the best of good company, as a host unsurpassed. It is said that he would have been Sir Samuel had he been a Churchman; but one can scarce believe that, in a land where religions are equal. Adelaide is a beautiful city, laid out with broad streets and public parks to the best advantage. It seemed to me, as I landed from the *Austral* and took the train at the end of the pier in Largs Bay, that I had got into as stale and sandy a bit of country as ever I saw in my life. However, appearances improved as I passed through the busy port and entered the city, which I like better the more I see of it. As you may imagine by the name, the place is of recent origin. It was founded in 1834, and in 1836 it became the residence of a governor, and then the site of the present city was fixed on. 'It is situated,' wrote one of the officials, 'on gently rising ground on both banks of a pretty stream, reaching down to the sea, over which south-west breezes blow nine months out of the twelve with invigorating freshness. At the back is a beautifully-wooded country, which extends for about six miles, to the first range of hills. The hills seem to surround the town, except where they melt, as it were, into the sand of the seashore.' The then existing woods, however, have been cut down, and all along the plain are the homes of the citizens. You see few fine houses—mostly they are small—one story—with iron roofs and little gardens, where the inhabitants grow a few flowers and spend their evenings under the veranda, smoking or reading, as it seems good in their eyes. In one of them I found an old friend whom I had not seen for forty-five years. 'Do you remember me?' I said. 'Yes,' was the reply, as he mentioned my name. The fact is, he had seen that I was in Australia by the newspapers, and he fully expected I would call. Alas! his wife was less quick in recognising my manly form. In Adelaide you see little of the rush and excitement which make Melbourne and Sydney famous. It has a university and educational endowments, and newspapers in abundance. Where I am located, I look out on the palm-trees which decorate the Governor's residence, and a little further on are the fine buildings known as the Public Library and Museum, and beyond them are the Botanical Gardens, well worthy of a visit, though less beautifully situated than those of Sydney. On my left is the railway-station and the new Houses of Parliament, and the road which leads down to the Torrens Lake, across which a handsome bridge has been thrown, and where the young athletes of the city spend their summer evenings. I walk up King William Street, with its Town Hall and Post-office, all white, as are most of the houses and grand offices in the wide streets, and pass Victoria Square, on the other side of which are the Law Courts. The buildings devoted to religious purposes are many, and in one of them preaches the Rev. R. Fletcher, a powerful-looking man intellectually, in the prime of life, and the principal of the new college the Congregationalists are about to establish. He gathers around him an influential and very respectable congregation (about a dozen of his hearers are Members of Parliament), but, like all the rest of the city pastors, both at home and in Australia, Mr. Fletcher finds yearly he loses old hearers, who move into the suburbs, and their vacant seats are left unoccupied. The Bishop of the city, Dr. Kennion, is highly spoken of. Here, as at home, and all over Australia, there are Christians of all sorts, nor are the members of the Salvation Army conspicuous by their absence. The dream of Christian unity seems in Australia as far off realization as at home. One Church parson with whom I have come in contact is a fine specimen of the muscular Christian. He is a canon of the Church, and is immensely popular as a preacher and a man. The following anecdote is characteristic: Once upon a time he was troubled at finding his stack of firewood rapidly diminishing. As it was not burnt in the house, he concluded it was taken off by a thief. To detect him was the proper thing, and the worthy canon sat for a night or two to wait for the enemy. Nor had he long to wait, as he appeared in the shape of a sailor. 'Now,' said the divine, 'we'll fight for it. If you beat me, I will let you off; if I beat you, I will give you in charge.' They did fight, and the sailor got such a licking as he never had before. 'Is the story true?' I said to the canon. He shook his head, and exclaimed, 'Ah, that's a sad tale!' Evidently in his heart he was proud of his pluck, and well he may be; many a one goes to hear him preach who would have kept away had he not been as ready with his fists as eloquent of tongue.

As I pass up King William Street, I see what is called the Royal Exchange. I enter, and behold an eager and excited mob. They are all men—most of them are smoking, in spite of an announcement to the effect that smoking is strictly forbidden. I point out the notice to one of the smokers, and he only smiles. What are they about? Buying and selling mining shares. This seems to be the leading industry of the place, and they buy and sell here to the extent of £300,000 or £400,000 a year. A broker explains to me that it is a safe way of making money if you are not frightened, but keep your shares, and if you deal with a broker who has no shares of his own to sell. 'If you do,' adds my informant, 'there is no telling what a mess you may be drawn into.' I thank him, and leave him, regretting that I have no money to invest, as I am certain to win if I take his kindly and disinterested advice. In the evening I find the business still in full swing. It is eight o'clock, and the Exchange is shut up, but my friend the broker is still playing his little game. He has changed the venue, that is all. I pass through a long passage at the end of an hotel; I descend a few steps, and am in a large room. On one side my friend stands in a Lilliputian rostrum, with his hammer in his hand. 'Now, gentlemen,' he says, 'now is your time—ten Junction Shares, buyer at eleven and three—seller at eleven and six—come on, gentlemen;' but the gentlemen don't seem much inclined to come on. They are a sleepy lot—leaning or sitting all round the room. At length says one of the crowd, 'I'll take that,' and the auctioneer's hammer rings sharply on the desk. And thus the evening wears away, till the lot is gone through. No one is excited—no large fortunes are here lost or won. Everything is on a small scale, and it is to be hoped that the buyers know what they are about. The auctioneer, a little man with a diamond ring glittering on his finger, evidently does. As to mines, all Adelaide is interested in them. In almost every shop you see specimens of ore displayed of some kind or other, no matter what the business of the shop may be. But, oh! the loveliness of the night as I reascend the steps, and leave the little knot of speculators behind. The shops are closed. The streets are almost deserted. There are no crowds of loafers and larrikins as in Melbourne or Sydney. There is scarce a living being at the bars besides the keeper or his girl. The shadows of the trees fall on the broad pavement. On the other side the white houses glisten in the moonlight, for the moon pours out a silvery flood of glory, almost hiding the stars of the blue sky above. It must be some such night as this that suggested the idea to the man who first ventured to speak of Holy Adelaide. Even the hills far away seem to live anew as they revive the silence and the splendour of a long-forgotten past.

In general intelligence, according to an interesting report just published by the Inspector - General of Victorian Schools—in general intelligence, the children of the large towns in the three colonies are very much alike. In New South Wales a higher standard is aimed at than in the other colonies. Victoria spends a considerable amount of money in establishing scholarships, so as to enable the most promising of State scholars to pass through the secondary schools; but in the senior colony Euclid, Algebra, and Latin or French form part of the ordinary course of instruction in the fifth class of the elementary public schools. The attempt is to do much—too much in too little time. In South Australia an opposite policy prevails. The teachers of the three colonies display on the whole equal industry and care. In the large city schools children over fourteen years of age show nearly equal proficiency in Victoria and South Australia in the ordinary subjects of primary instruction, and rather less in New South Wales. Children about thirteen are about equal in the three colonies. Children between eleven and twelve are the most proficient in South Australia, and the least in Victoria. If attainments in Algebra, Euclid, Latin, and French are taken into account, New South Wales has the best results to show. In New South Wales the teachers are paid a fixed salary. In Victoria the system of payment by results is wholly, in South Australia partially, adopted. Observations tend to show that the bad effect of payment by results is quite as conspicuous where the system prevails as where it does not.

In 1829 England was taking rather a rosy view of the unfortunate Swan River Settlement. It ended, as most of us know, in disastrous failure. But it was put before the public in an attractive form, or we should not find the great Dr. Arnold writing from Rugby to his friend the Rev. I. Tucker: 'If we are alive fifteen years hence I think I would go gladly to Swan River if they will make me schoolmaster there, and lay my bones in the land of kangaroos and opossums. My notion is that no missionizing is half so beneficial as to try to pour sound and healthy blood into a young civilized society, to make one colony, if possible, like the ancient colonies in New England—a living sucker from the mother country, bearing the same blossoms and the same fruits; not a reproduction of its vilest excrescences, its ignorance, while all the good qualities are left behind in the process. No words can tell the evil of such colonies as we have hitherto planted, where the best parts of the new society have been men too poor to carry with them or to gain much of the higher branches of knowledge, or else mere official functionaries from England, whose hearts and minds have been always half at home, and who have never identified themselves with the land in which they were working.' Arnold did well to remain where he was. In the Swan Colony immense blocks of land were freely granted to settlers, regardless of their means to profitably occupy such holdings. As a consequence, the farmers had no labourers to till the soil, and many of the large estates lay waste, or only supported a few head of cattle. It was in South Australia, if anywhere, an attempt was made to realize Dr. Arnold's ideal. It was started on the Wakefield system, which worked well for a time, and attracted the right men into the land. It was resolved that it should be free from the taint of felony, and it was resolved that it should have no State Church ; and the spirit of the founders still permeates the land. At any rate, in Adelaide I found better society than I did anywhere else.

Leaving Adelaide on my way home, I must speak of a few of the blots of Australian life. When Paul tells us he fought with beasts at Ephesus, we feel inclined to pity the unfortunate saint; but when people talk of mosquitoes that is quite another matter, and yet I know not whether it is worst to fight with beasts at Ephesus than to wrestle with mosquitoes all through the watches of the night, as I did at Melbourne. At Sydney I was told they would worry me to death, but there they left me unharmed. At Melbourne I was informed, on unexceptionable authority, that the mosquitoes would not annoy me at all, and it was with a light heart that I went to bed, little dreaming that I should rise a sadder and a wiser man on the morrow—a spectacle for gods and men—with all the blood sucked out of my body, and prematurely gray. I know that I am a sinner; I know that I have done the things which I ought not to have done, and left undone the things which I should have done; I know (as Shakespeare tells us) if we all had our deserts there would be none of us who would escape whipping; I have written, I own, a good deal of indifferent prose and poetry, have kept late hours, and have seen a good deal of the wicked world—a moderate amount of punishment I am prepared for. 'What a man soweth that shall he also reap,' is a law that runs through life, and for wise and salutary ends. But it was hard, nevertheless, to have to fight with such paltry, insignificant creatures as mosquitoes—mere stings on Lilliputian wings, too ridiculous to be considered as enemies—yet I own they kept me awake all one night, as they tortured me from the crown of my head to the sole of my foot, and made me tremble and perspire as I heard them trumpeting previous to a general attack as I never had done before. I never felt so savage; I never saw my poor body so cut up with scars. I was to dine next day with one of the handsomest ladies in Melbourne, a fine specimen of an Irish beauty, to whom I was anxious to present myself in as respectable a plight as possible ; but all was of no avail. Mercifully, however, the brutes so gorged themselves that I was enabled to take a righteous revenge ; but it was an awful night, and I felt how David must have had them in his eye when he longed, in one of his grand psalms, for the wings of a dove, to fly away and be at rest.

Alas, alas! if we have the mosquitoes by night, there are also flies which are a real terror by day, especially in places of worship, where they seriously interfere alike with the inattentive or the attentive hearer. They don't seem to interest themselves much in the preliminary part of the service—they are conspicuous by their absence in singing and chanting, and there is a good deal of both in Australia—but immediately the text is announced and you have settled yourself down in an attitude of repose the attack commences. At first you heed it not—it seems too ridiculous to be bothered by a fly. At last your blood boils, and you can stand it no longer. The tiny tormentor flies into your mouth, should it perchance be open, settles on the most sensitive part of your nose, assails your forehead, attacks your ears, and every other vulnerable point. You give a bang, but you have missed your mark; your enemy is beyond your reach, only to return with fresh vigour to the attack. Not a moment does he leave you at rest; not a moment can you listen in peace and comfort; not a moment, while the sermon lasts, are you in a proper, Christian frame of mind. When I went to hear Dr. Strong, the great Australian heretic, the fly—for providentially, as a rule, it is only one fly that attacks you at a time—was especially active. That fly must have belonged to the ranks of the orthodox, and thought I deserved little mercy for once in my lifetime straying from the fold. At any rate, little mercy he showed to me. A minor nuisance is the Australian cricket, which commences to make an extraordinary row as the sun goes down. Another nuisance are the song-birds, as they call them. Sitting one day in the Sydney Botanical Gardens—very beautiful, but not so fine as those of Melbourne—I was startled as if all the grinding machinery in the colony had been put in motion to set my teeth on edge. 'What's that?' I asked in alarm. 'Only the birds singing,' was the somewhat unsatisfactory reply.

An interesting table has been published which purports to give the Drink Bill of Australasia for 1887. The statement has been prepared by the Victorian

Alliance, and although it is not easy to conjecture how some of the information has been obtained, it may at least be assumed from its authorship that the amount of the Bill has not been kept unreasonably low. Assuming it to be correct, we find that the several colonies spent £15,582,485 on their liquor in 1887, representing an outlay of £4 8s. 6d. for each man, woman, and child alive in that year. Western Australia spent more in proportion to her population than any of her sister colonies, her bill amounting to £6 10s. per head. Next comes Queensland at a respectable distance, with £5 9s. 4d. per head, closely followed by Victoria with £5 5s. New South Wales pays £4 10s. 3d., Tasmania, £3 6s. 7d., and New Zealand, £3 5s. South Australia modestly brings up the rear with an average payment per head of only £2 19s.

Sunday in Adelaide is the *beau idéal* of the Puritan Sabbath. The other Australian cities attempt something of the kind, but in Adelaide the thing has been achieved, and except for Christian workers in the pulpit or the Sunday-school the day is emphatically one of rest. Somehow or other the Sunday seems in keeping with the place. At no time does Adelaide strike you as a city of business. The air is too pure, the sky too lovely, the streets too clean. About lunch time there seems to be a little pressure in the streets, and a little business in the shops; at the club we are quite full at that sacred hour, and under the veranda in the tiny square behind, where we boast a couple of fern palms, a fountain, and one gold fish, the smokers congregate, while the click of the balls indicates the presence of company in the billiard-room adjoining. But to-day the only people about are the church-goers. I followed the crowd to the Stowe Memorial Church, in Flinders Street. The Rev. Thomas Quinton Stowe, who was born at Hadleigh, in Suffolk, must have had much to do with the building up of the Adelaide of to-day. The church of which he was the pastor was established at a meeting held in a tent, provided by the Colonial Missionary Society, in December, 1837, with Mr. Stowe for its first pastor. The next building was a sanctuary of pine and reeds, erected in North Terrace. The church grew with the growth of the colony, and in 1840 removed to a large square building in Freeman Street. There Mr. Stowe remained till advancing age hinted retirement. In 1862 he died, leaving behind him the useful memory of a devoted life. No name is more connected with the religious history of the colony. He was trusted by all for his sincerity, honoured for his wisdom, respected for his talents, and beloved for his piety. The Church, wishing to commemorate his name, and being in need of a new and larger place of assembly, built the Stowe Memorial Church, the foundation-stone of which was laid in 1865 by the Hon. Alexander Hay, and which was opened for public worship in 1867. It is a large and handsome building, erected in Flinders Street, where the Presbyterians and Baptists also have places of worship. It was a relief to turn into it, when I was there, out of the scorching sun. There is no gallery, but the area is very large, and the buildings in connection with the place are numerous, and ornamental as well as useful. They consist of a lecture-hall, a schoolroom, and attendant class-rooms. In 1876 the Rev. Wm. Roby Fletcher, of Richmond, Melbourne, accepted the call of the people and became pastor. It was at his handsome home, a little way out of town—surrounded by books and curios—that I supped after the evening service. His wife is an Australian lady. He is specially learned in Indian subjects, where he was sent by the Government to study its educational system, and from which he has not long returned. In Adelaide Mr. Fletcher occupies high rank.

One thing that may be said of him is that he is ready to utilise passing events. In the week there had been a tragedy in Adelaide of a very painful character. There had been a fire in a temperance coffee-palace, and of the guests a Mr. Taplin had been burnt to death. Mr. Taplin was a fine, stalwart man, of imposing presence, and well-known to the public as the head of the Point Macleay Mission to the Blacks, which was founded by his father, the Rev. G. Taplin. The father was one of the first arrivals in the colony, and meeting a black-fellow as he stepped ashore, he conceived the idea that with religious and industrial training something might be done with the aborigines. He lost no time or opportunity in giving practical effect to his convictions, and in due time he found himself superintendent of the Aboriginal Farm and Mission Station, where he toiled till his death in 1879, having in the meantime wrought a wonderful improvement in the condition of the blacks, and exhibited many proofs of the controverted point that the aborigines are capable of receiving and understanding a higher form of spiritual knowledge than that in which they were bred. The blacks loved him with their whole hearts, and admired him as a sort of demigod. One of them, when questioned by a carping critic as to the existence of a Deity, replied, 'You know Massa Taplin, and then you no fear plenty believe'n God.'

The senior Mr. Taplin was not only a practical agriculturist, architect, and jack-of-all-trades, as it were, but he was as well a man of much learning and piety. His acquaintance with the art of healing was only equalled by his deep knowledge of Australian philology. When the father died he was succeeded by his son William, who, though he dropped the title of reverend, followed in his father's steps. He was a Catholic Christian, excelling in preaching as much as in the physical exercises of the natives. He was recognised as public vaccinator of the district. In the harder manual work he kept abreast of the times, and only recently the Mission Committee undertook, under his direction, to carry out some much-needed irrigation work on the reserve. He had come to Adelaide to discuss with the committee the concerns of the mission, and he gave a lecture before the Australian Natives Association, on 'Our Aboriginals: Their Manners and Customs; or, a Native Fifty Years Ago.' He overslept himself, and that necessitated another night in Adelaide; and then came the tragic end, all the more tragical as he was the only one of the guests who knew the way of escape, which leads to the supposition that he must have lost his own life in saving the lives of others. It was on his death that Mr. Fletcher based his discourse. It was listened to by a congregation attentive and highly respectable as regards appearance. As to the church itself: inside it is very spacious, and, not being disfigured by galleries, presents almost a cathedral-like appearance. In the evening I heard from afar the band of the Salvation Army. They are in Adelaide as everywhere else. I should have thought that the Army might have been more usefully employed elsewhere. 'You can't go far in Adelaide,' said a man in the street to me, 'without seeing a church. There are about four in every street.' Perhaps this explains the fact why Adelaide is called 'holy.' Alas! in England we often say, 'the nearer the church the further from God!'

CHAPTER VIII.

LIFE AT A STATION.

Mr. Dooleete's Station — Sheep-shearing — Patriarchal Life improved — Snakes — Drought.

I DID not see much of station life in Australia. I was to have visited Mr. Angas's in South Australia, one of the show-places of the colony, but the heat prevented me. However, Mr. Dooleete, of Adelaide, very kindly took me to one he has in conjunction with a friend, about 100 miles from Adelaide, and I much enjoyed the trip. We started early in the morning from Mr. Dooleete's romantic residence among the hills, and were swiftly carried to the junction where the Melbourne train arrives. From here we were to take with us a gentleman who was purchasing horses for the Indian Government, Australia having a breed of horses particularly suited for our cavalry out there. A gentleman in Adelaide told me, when his father was a Congregational minister at Bury St. Edmund's, in Suffolk, he persuaded the eccentric Rowland Hill to come and preach for him. There being no Great Eastern Railway in those days, Mr. Hill travelled, as was his wont, in his carriage and pair, and was naturally anxious as to who was to look after his horses.

'Oh,' said the minister, 'they will be taken care of by a member of my church—a horse-dealer.'

'What!' said Rowland Hill, lifting up his hands in amazement; 'a horse-dealer a member of a Christian Church! who ever heard of such a thing?'

The horse-dealer who joined our party was, if not a member of a Christian Church, at any rate a particularly good judge of a horse, and was at once able to recognise the animal he considered useful for his work.

It was a pretty country through which we travelled. Here and there we came to a station, around which was rising up a small town; but mainly we saw nothing but forest and scrub with few signs of life. We stopped at a small town situated on Lake Alexandrina, and, after lunching at an hotel kept by a worthy colonist from Essex, who seemed perfectly contented with his lot, we got on board a small yacht, the management of which was left to bulky blacks belonging to the mission station at Port Macleay, on the other side. A small crowd of black children greeted us on our landing, and then we climbed up into a commodious waggonette drawn by two horses, and in a couple of hours had reached the end of our journey. All the way neither house nor road was to be seen. On our left was the lake, far ahead was the Murray River, and on our right seemed to be a grand park many miles in extent, only a little more parched-looking than a park at home, and everywhere strewed with trees that had fallen, which would have fetched a good price for firewood in the towns if they could be got there. There were sheep by the hundred, and there were horses roaming, as it were, monarchs of all they surveyed. The scene was slightly monotonous. Now and then we came to a rough fence, through the gates of which we had to make our way, and I was not sorry when we dashed up to a handsome residence on the brow of a hill commanding a fine view of the lake. We had brought with us a respectable young woman, who was to wait on us, and a good supply of eatables, so that my fears on that important head were soon set at rest. One does hear strange stories of life at a station. I heard of a colonial governor who, meeting one of the original squatters in the enjoyment of all the luxury of a Melbourne Club, asked him how, after that, he could put up with such lenten fare at home. He replied to the effect that the governor was quite mistaken—the squatters did live well; and, by way of clinching his contention, he went on to state that he had repeatedly seen at the same time on the table both sardines and pickles! I think we had neither, but we lived as luxuriously as in any gentleman's house either in the colony or at home. We had the best of everything, and the place was furnished in the most sumptuous manner, including even a piano, which must have come a long way, and which could find but little to do, as the house was only open when we were there, and was again locked up as we drove away. Visitors are rare in that part of the world; and as to the doctor, if his services were required, the patient would have to wait a good while. Death, or, what is more likely, recovery, might occur before the doctor could arrive. There was little time to lose and early in the morning Mr. Dooleete and his friend were driving in a buggy across the plain to look at the horses. After I had had my breakfast I toiled down in the sun to where the sheep were penned in previous to being partially shorn. They had all been driven in the night before, and the men—blacks, who had come from the missionary station, with their wives and little ones —were lodged in tents on the shore of the lake. They were stout and dull-looking, with wives, as a rule, still stouter and duller-looking, with the exception of one young woman—a very pretty half-breed.

A white man was the superintendent, and he had a dry and dusty time of it as he did his duty—that is, divide the sheep, the Merinos from the Leicesters, I believe. First, they had to be driven into yards— and here the sheep-dogs were specially serviceable—till they were all collected, to the number, if I remember aright, of five or six thousand (of course, they were not all in one pen); then they were driven along a little lane, fenced in, where the superintendent stood at a double gate, to divide the sheep according to their breed. This was done by blocking one gate and opening the other side as the sheep approached. Thus separated, they were taken, a few at a time, into the shearing-shed, a large brick building, with the sheep in the middle and the shearers on each side. Operations were at once commenced. The shearer selects his animal, holds it up between his legs, and quickly cuts off the wool, which is swept off the stone floor by women, who separate it and put it into sacks, while the frightened animal, released from the grasp of his persecutor, bounds through an opening in the wall and rejoins his companions who have undergone a similar process. It is warm work this, and every now and then the workman stops to have a drink of water—a beverage available, fortunately, to any amount. As soon as the sheep are shorn, the wool is packed up and sent off to market. A small steamer, which goes slowly up and down the lake, is thus utilised for commercial purposes. I returned by that steamer. It may be sure; it certainly is slow. Being at this station was a vastly pleasant change to me. I had had quite enough of city life. It may be very lonely to live on that hill, in that fine house, with no neighbours with whom to chat, far from shops and post-office and newspapers; but with books and one's family it must be a noble existence. There may be stormy winds out there, for I saw many a fine tree blown down; but mostly the country round rejoices in blue skies and an unclouded sun. In that region there is no particular chance of overcrowding at any rate, just at present. The worst of the squatter is that he does not require much labour. A very few hands suffice for him—except at the shearing season —to look after his flocks and herds. You realize in such a place something of the life of the Patriarchs, only considerably improved. The owner of a station must spend a good deal of his time in the saddle, and a horse, I imagine, is infinitely to be preferred to the camel. The noble steed enjoys himself as he springs along the turf. At all times, whether lying down or rising up, whether loaded or not, whether ungainly walking or hideously trotting, a camel is a picture of bitter woefulness and abject despair. The station, too, has its innocent amusements. I have a friend who has a station about a hundred miles from Melbourne. To him came when I was there a city gentleman, who betted that he would kill a hundred snakes within the hour, and he shot ninety-eight! A fond mother who lives in a fine station in New South Wales, told me how once upon a time she had to snatch away her little one sleeping on the lawn, as a black snake had crept up to within a foot of its precious head. Then there is a drought, and your flocks have to be taken miles to water. After all, there is plenty of excitement—for those who seek it— even in station life.

CHAPTER IX.

THE HEATHEN CHINEE.

His Persecution—His Usefulness—His Intellectual Ability.

THE Chinese in Australia have a grievance. We have opened up China against the wishes of their rulers, and when they take a leaf out of our book, and commence opening up the world, we turn round and refuse them admission. It is so in America, and it is so in Australia. At every election meeting in Victoria when I was there, the candidate had to declare that he was ready to vote for the exclusion of the Chinese. This is how democracy uses its power. The Chinaman is civil, and obliging, and hard-working; besides, he is sober; but the Australians won't have him at any price, and raise the cry of Australia for the Australians, which means that no poor English emigrant may go there to take lower wages than his mates rather than starve at home. As each colony is isolated, this will mean in time that the work of each colony is to be done only by its own workmen. Already in Queensland I see that a complaint has been made because some workmen from Sydney have been brought in to work. Australia wants opening up. It has only a sparse population on its borders, and in many parts the workman, who is master of the situation, will not work himself, nor allow any one else to do so. The general public suffer, but that is their look-out. Prices are kept up by Protection, and the protected further protect themselves by keeping out the labourer anxious to earn an honest living. As the Chinese are weak and friendless, it is against them chiefly that this policy is enforced. I heard one day of a sturdy workman who had applied for relief. When asked what he had been doing of late, he replied that he had been picking grapes. Questioned why he had given the occupation up, he answered that he was working with Chinese, and the boss expected him to work as hard as they did.

Australia wants to compete with the cheap wine-sellers of Bordeaux; but she is sadly handicapped in this and other ways. The farmer finds his corn-fields eaten up by the parroquets, because he can hire no cheap labour to scare away the birds. In the big towns it is the Chinaman who supplies the people with cheap fish and vegetables. I own to a liking for the 'heathen Chinee.' 'Ah,' said a well-known London Democrat to me after I had returned home, 'I see what you want. You want to reduce the British workman to the level of the heathen Chinee.' 'No,' was my reply. 'I want to bring the British workman up to the level of the heathen Chinee. He is economical, industrious, sober, and always civil, and one cannot say that in all cases of the British workman.' And in the northern district they are sadly wanted. While in Adelaide, I read a letter in *The South Australian Register*, in which the writer emphatically declares that if any development of the northern territory is to take place, it must be by the Chinese, or not at all. The writer remarks : 'If the Chinese are excluded or kept out here, all development will cease, and the northern territory will just resolve itself into a great Government camp, where some will be employed to watch the telegraph wires, while others are scraping the rust off the wheels of the railway carriages.' And then he goes on to speak of the bogus telegrams and Munchausen reports that caused the Chinese scare. This northern territory, be it remembered, which has been tacked on to South Australia and governed from Adelaide, embraces an immense extent of country,

and contains an area of about 323,620 square miles.
Its principal harbour is Port Darwin, which is one of
the finest in Australia, almost equalling that of Sydney.
It is rich in mineral resources, and gold and rubies.
The climate is tropical, and the soil in many parts is
very rich. Already it contains many great cattle
stations. The writer I have referred to says : ' I have
had a nearly three years' residence here, trying to
develop a large run for a Victorian owner. This
enables me to speak with complete knowledge of the
climate, and the kind of labour suitable for the
country; for out-of-door work the European may be
dismissed at once.' Clearly, in such a case, the
Chinaman is the right man in the right place. But
'No,' say the Queenslanders; 'if you allow the
Chinese there, they will cross the border and come to
us.' Again, says an intelligent Adelaide editor to
me: 'It cannot be; the Chinese are many, we are
few — they will take possession of all Australia.'
Surely it would not be a difficult thing to limit the
extent of Chinese immigration. A Chinaman cannot
disguise his nationality. Dress him in Christian
clothes—his *tout ensemble*, his oval face, his brown
skin, his high cheek-bones, his little twinkling eyes,
will betray him, to say nothing of his pigtail and his
pigeon English. By all means, in the interests of

civilization, I would say, let him come. It would be better for Australia and the world that it should be opened up, than allowed to remain a waste.

In Adelaide I have seen a splendid specimen of what a Chinaman may become when he is naturalized and turned into a British subject. His name is Mr. Way Lee, and a more agreeable man I have not seen for a long time. His shop was full of China ware and Chinese tea. He had on a black coat, a white waistcoat, a light pair of trousers, and his pigtail was rolled into a neat plait at the back of his head. In his drawing-room he had a piano, and a portrait of her Majesty in a very rich gold frame. His only peculiarity of costume was as regards his small feet, which were encased in Chinese slippers. He offered me a glass of wine much as an ordinary Christian would have done; I refused it, but, however, accepted a Manilla cheroot, and we got into a pleasant talk. He told me that he was thirty-seven; I should have guessed that he was not more than twenty-five. He had two extraordinary, highly-coloured religious Chinese pictures, which made me believe that he was a follower of Confucius. However, I was deceived. 'I go,' said he, with a bland smile, 'to the Baptist, the Congregational, the Wesleyan Churches—any vere my friends take me.'

Not a bigot, at any rate, is Mr. Way Lee. In Adelaide he has won golden opinions. He has traded there for years; is straightforward in all his doings; has deservedly gained the reputation of being an exemplary citizen—strict in his regard for municipal rights and regulations, and vigilant in his endeavours to enforce the maintenance of law and order. And his own Government have conferred upon him the dignity of a Mandarin. He is renowned for his charity. Well, he has succeeded in business, and has an establishment in Sydney which, naturally, he desires to visit, but by crossing the border into New South Wales he renders himself liable to a heavy fine of £100. He has written to Sir Henry Parkes on the subject, but the Free Trade Premier tells him he cannot help him. Why, asks the paper which has taken, and rightly taken, up his case, should Mr. Way Lee, who has established as strong a claim upon the goodwill of his fellows, and the protection of the State as any of his trade competitors, be placed at a serious disadvantage in carrying on his business, because he happens to have been born in the Flowery Land? Why should he be held up to the ridicule and scorn of his fellow colonists because he hails from China? The time will come when Australia will be heartily ashamed of conduct which savours more of the narrow and intolerant spirit of the dark ages than of the enlightenment and liberality of modern times. There are not many such decent Chinese in Australia. Whose fault is that? Certainly the Caucasian has set the heathen Chinee a very sorry example. 'Government have inspectors,' said Way Lee to me; 'Government can put them down if they gamble and be wicked.' Surely the Caucasian can take care of himself; at any rate, he has the credit of being able to do so. The little almond-eyed heathen cheats him when he is drunk; then let him keep sober. I have been in an opium den; I have been in a gin-palace. The opium den is a heaven compared with the latter. In Australia every drunken larrikin thinks it good fun to push down or ill-treat a Chinee. Such brutality makes one's blood boil. Nor can it be well with a people where such ruffianism exists in its midst. Australia is big, and so big that the Australians themselves are little acquainted with it. Surely there is room enough for the Chinaman, and he can open up such parts of it as are unhealthy for the European. Mr. Way Lee, in every respect, is as good an Australian as any I have met with; his manners are unexceptionable; he goes into society. Such as he do not level down, but are levelled up, and Australia might do with China a large and profitable trade. I question whether the leaders in the anti-Chinese crusade are really in earnest; they join in it as a means to an end; by means of it they trust to get place and power. All I could do was to assure Mr. Lee that we in England were not responsible for such treatment as he had received; that we had little else to do than to supply the colonies with governors and a fleet. 'Yes, I know,' he said; but he felt the hardship, nevertheless.

Intellectually the heathen Chinee is coming to the front. In describing the results of recent examinations at the University of Melbourne, a newspaper writer says: 'Dr. Bevan's eldest son (Willett) carried off no less than nine prizes at the Church of England Grammar School, including the Dux and Speaker's Prize, another son of the doctor's also doing well. It is not without satirical suggestion, however, that Cheong (who was second Dux) beat Bevan in English spelling and New Testament Greek. It is curious, to say the least of it, that a Chinese should excel an English boy in *English* spelling, and that the son of a convert from heathenism should surpass the son of a Christian pastor in an examination upon the text-book of the Christian faith.'

As to the usefulness of the Chinee in Australia I am glad to supplement my remarks with an extract from a letter of a gentleman in the *London and China Express.*

The writer, Mr. Sampson, an intelligent resident of many years in China, says : 'During a recent visit to Victoria, during which I made it my particular business to inquire into matters connected with the Chinese, I found that the objection to Chinese immigration is by no means universal in that colony. The principal objectors are the labour-aristocracy and the politicians who seek to gain their votes ; on the other side are the employers of labour generally—farmers, fruit-growers, masters of steamers, women burdened with domestic cares, and sometimes even diggers and unskilled labourers, who are not bound to accept the doctrines dictated by a labour union. "We don't want the Chinese to go," said a labouring man to me, at a wayside inn, some ten miles from Sandhurst ; he was an Irishman, and was celebrating the news of the defeat of the *Times* in the matter of the forged letters. "We don't want the Chinese to go ; we want them to stop here, and grow cabbages for us." This pithily-expressed view of the question I found very prevalent. A lady fellow-passenger in a steamer said to me, with a sigh, " Ah, if women had votes there would be no restrictions on the immigration of Chinese." She valued them as faithful and dutiful domestic servants, and as polite, obliging, and honest hawkers of vegetables and other small household requirements. I visited a large orchard in which every grape had been sucked dry by birds, and the parrots were making sad havoc amongst the apples, pears, and peaches. I remarked to the owner that in China a couple of men could be employed to keep away the birds at ten shillings a month. "Ah!" was the reply. "Here I should have to pay eight shillings a day, and then I should have to stay on the grounds myself to see that they did their work." The following characteristic story was told me: An Australian, being about to leave the colony for a year or two, instructed a broker to let for that period a piece of land which he owned. The broker secured a tenant, and the owner agreed to the terms without inquiring who the tenant was. When the time arrived for him to sign the legal documents he found that the proposed tenant was a Chinaman. He wished to repudiate the bargain, but matters had advanced too far for him to do so. On his return from England he found that the Chinese tenant had improved the ground so much that he said, "If ever I have to go away again I will let a Chinaman have the use of my land for nothing rather than accept rent from a white man." These anecdotes are, of course, only isolated cases, but they serve to illustrate opinions, and to show forth facts of importance.'

CHAPTER X.

THE LARRIKIN IN AUSTRALIA.

What the Larrikin is—A Social, Moral, and Political Danger—A Natural Foe of the Chinaman.

ONCE upon a time, so the story runs, an old gentleman was walking along the streets of London, when he was accosted by a little boy, who asked him for a light for his cigarette. The old gentleman, of course, was shocked, and indignantly remarked that when he was young little boys were not allowed to smoke. 'Oh,' replied the lad, 'there ain't any boys now; they are all young men; that's what we call 'em, and old men we call thundering fools.' This feeling, unfortunately, exists wherever there are civilized men and women. In savage countries it may be that the hoary head is a crown of honour; but where the schoolmaster has gone abroad the first impression made on the mind of the favoured scholar is that he is a man and his father but a fool. Old customs, old traditions, somewhat interfere with this idea in English towns and villages, yet the increasing tendency of the age is in another direction. All kindly correction has been denied the youth, especially of the working-classes. Let the lad ever so richly deserve a flogging, father or mother threatens 'if you dare to lay a hand upon my boy,' and so the master spares the rod and spoils the child. In some quarters the boy soon begins to earn his living, and then he spends his wages and his time in bad company, and is a terror to father and mother, and master, and all with whom he has to do. It is to this phase of civilization is due, in that highly-favoured country of Australia, the existence of the larrikin. It was while I was out there that there died the policeman who invented the name. In the course of his arduous duties he had to catch and bring before the magistrates a group of troublesome lads. 'What were they doing?' asked the magistrates. 'I caught them a-larrikin,' was the reply, and ever since then the name of larrikin denotes a lad in a hobbledehoy state, who is a torment to himself and everyone around. Worst of all, the chances are that he develops into a rough, and brutal, and unmannerly man. As it is, he is a nuisance everywhere, but a special danger in Australia in a social, and moral, and political point of view. In a new country naturally the young people assert themselves more than in an old one. You see this in America as well as in Australia, but in the latter country the press does its duty and points out the danger. In one of the best of the Australian papers—*The South Australian Register*—a leader-writer, in recommending the volunteer movement, remarks that there is no hardship in asking the Australian young man to take his place among the defenders of his country. On the contrary it would be of great physical and moral benefit to him to undergo the training of a citizen soldier. 'Impatience of control, lack of discipline, a contempt for authority, the absence of a sense of duty—these are the prevailing faults of the youth of the day, and it is certain that a course of military exercises would have a bracing effect upon the moral nature, helping to make the young men better sons, better husbands, better fathers—in every way better qualified to discharge the important functions of responsible citizens in a State where all possess equal political rights and perfect freedom of action.' As I write I read in a New South Wales paper: 'Larrikinism is on the increase in the suburbs of Brisbane. Constant complaints are made of insults to pedestrians, drunken quarrels and profane language. On Sunday the hotels a short distance from the city are visited, and under the influence of the potations indulged in the most unholy scenes of rioting and revelling take place on the roads. Church-goers are subjected to insult. Decent parents are obliged to shut their children within doors to prevent their ears being assailed by the oaths and curses freely uttered by these lawless pests. The police generally are nowhere to be seen, and when present are indisposed to arrest the offenders. Our laws are badly applied.'

The larrikin is the natural foe of the heathen Chinee; not that he dislikes his imputed vices, but his real virtues. A friend of mine was walking near the suburbs of Melbourne, and he came across a Chinaman working in his garden, where only parsley was growing. 'How is this?' said my friend. 'Why don't you grow vegetables and flowers? I should have thought they would have paid you better.' 'Ah, sir,' replied the heathen, 'if I were to grow vegetables and flowers, the larrikins would come and pull them all up; so I can only grow parsley.' And thus the people of Melbourne suffer, for those of them who have no gardens of their own have to depend for their supplies on the ever civil and industrious Chinamen. Since I have returned home, I see a Melbourne judge declared that it was unsafe to walk the streets of Melbourne by night or by day, and that that is so is, I take it, mainly due to the larrikins, who exist in such numbers as to defy the power of the police. When a larrikin gets drunk and quarrelsome he naturally goes in for the Chinese; they are few, and he and his friends are many. They are fond of fighting, and a Chinaman is a man of peace. It is fine sport for the larrikin to trample down and devastate the well-kept garden of the heathen Chinee, to get into his little shop and spoil his goods, to knock about and ill-treat the son of the Celestial Empire; nor does he object to murder one if he has the chance, as probably by means of perjury and hard swearing he will be able to escape the punishment due to his crime. By night the larrikins sleep in the parks, which are the glory of all the Australian cities, and the scenes there, so I was informed, are disgraceful. It is not safe for a respectable person to walk across the parks alone of a night. As in London, almost all respectable people live out of town, and they have but a faint idea of what goes on in their absence. The climate allows anyone, at any rate during the summer months, to sleep in the open air, and the rascals of the community for the time being may each one say for himself:

> 'I am monarch of all I survey,
> My right there is none to dispute.'

It is one of the drawbacks of the Australian climate that it gives the larrikin a chance such as he has nowhere else. Walking one evening with a friend in one of the parks which adorn Adelaide, we came to a young tree which had the bark cut off in a circle round the trunk—in other words, it was ring-barked. My friend indignantly exclaimed: 'See what the larrikins have been up to!' That tree was doomed to die. It was a valuable one. It had been planted for a special purpose—to add to the attractions of the park, and to be, when fully grown, a benefit to the entire community. It had leaves on. It did not seem to have suffered much damage; but it was doomed to die, nevertheless. As a resident in Adelaide, my friend was very much provoked at the sight; and no wonder.

Wherever you go you meet the detestable larrikin, but it is in Melbourne that he chiefly abounds. Fathers and mothers are much to be blamed on his account. There is an old commandment about honouring thy father and mother, to which, if I were a Melbourne parson, I should devote many sermons; but, alas! in a young community, with many questionable emigrants, where the fever of gold-getting in any way rages fiercely, it is not always that a young man can honour his father and mother. At any rate, the evil exists, and Church and State between them will have hard work to put it down. The larrikin delights in mischief for mischief's sake. He is not necessarily very poor or wretched. Perhaps he gets too much flesh meat, and a vegetarian diet would suit him better. Dr. Dale tells us a good deal of the high spirits of the Australian youth—a phase of Australian life which did not strike me at all. Was he thinking of the Australian larrikin? Such high spirits are not to my taste. In one respect the larrikin reminds one of the days of Tom and Jerry as depicted in the vivid caricatures of the late George Cruikshank, but Tom and Jerry were gentlemen, and that makes a great difference. Rather I should take him to be a son of Belial, and thus give him a more ancient origin. His delight is to join himself to a gang of twenty or thirty to break street lamps, to wrench off knockers, tear down fences, mob and maltreat policemen, hustle respectable people at all hours by day and by night, and to assault some poor pedestrian, especially when a little the worse for liquor, and rob him. 'Scarce a week passes,' says a writer in the Colonies, 'without some larrikin outbreak.' It was even with difficulty that I could steer clear of him at times. I fear we have too much of the larrikin at home, but that is no reason why he should be allowed to taint the virgin soil of a new world. Our colonies ought to be an improvement on the old country. What is wrong at home they should avoid. Let them imitate our virtues. On a new soil they have a better chance.

CHAPTER XI.

IN AN AUSTRALIAN VINEYARD.

Fruit Supply—Tintarra Wine—Mr. Thomas Hardy—The Temperance Question.

ONE of the charms of South Australia is the fruit, which, in the shape of grapes, and pears, and peaches, and apples, you see everywhere displayed, and at astonishingly low prices. Grapes are sold at five pounds for sixpence in the retail shops, and I have seen magnificent grapes three pounds for sixpence, which in London would be held cheap at half-a-crown. If the colony is ever to be very rich, its fruit trade will be no inconsiderable factor in the consummation so devoutly to be wished. The farmer and the squatter have to contend with difficulties which often end in bankruptcy, owing to the terrible droughts common in this part of the world. But if the merchants of Adelaide will send us their spare fruit, we in London

In an Australian Vineyard. 193

can take any amount and at very remunerative prices. I saw during my tour the vineyards of Mr. Thomas Hardy, within a short distance of Adelaide, and I must own that the place is well worth a visit. Though of small extent (the area is only 60 acres), Bankside, as the vineyard is called, yields a more varied produce, and furnishes a better illustration of the capabilities of the soil and climate of the district in which it is situated, than any other estate in Australia. Mr. Hardy is a fine specimen of a horticulturist, and well deserves the splendid silver trophy which ornaments his drawing-room—and of which he is justly proud—given him as one who has done more than anyone in the colony to develop its resources. He has made good use of his grapes. We are not all teetotalers, and he grows more grapes on his various estates than the Australians can eat, whether as grapes for dessert, or in the shape of raisins and currants. With the rest he makes wine. He is proud of his wine—proud of the fact that even at Bordeaux, in the heart of the enemy's country, as it were, he won a gold medal for its excellence; proud of the fact that his celebrated Tintara wine has found a good place in the London market. As I have seen it manufactured I can testify as to its purity. He was sending this year 45,000 gallons to London. He would prefer to keep it longer in his cellars, but the Londoners want it, and he cannot keep them waiting. Why not sell the original grapes? asks the teetotaler. I reply, He grows more grapes than the community can devour with a decent regard to its health, and as people exist who are mistaken enough to think Paul was right when he recommended Timothy a little wine for his stomach's sake and his often infirmities, Mr. Hardy thinks he is a public benefactor if he supplies the public with a genuine wine, the produce of the grape and of the grape alone.

Mr. Hardy is no ignoramus; he is a much-travelled man, and has studied the vineyards of France and Spain and California. In his establishment he uses the best machinery—which of course is French—for the distillation of the purest and strongest spirits of wine, to which purpose such grapes are devoted as are not good enough for the production of wine of the best quality. As to the manufacture of wine, that is a very simple affair. The grapes are picked and placed in carts, and carried to the mill, where they lie fermenting in a mass; the juice is then pressed off into slate vats, a brown and by no means attractive-looking fluid. The red wines take longer to ferment, as the outside skin contains the colouring matter. In the case of the white grapes, the stalks are cut away by a machine invented for the purpose, otherwise the astringency of the wine would be too great. After a time the juice is put into casks, where it lies stored in cool and capacious cellars till it is required by the outside public. In some of the casks I saw the wine had been kept ten or twelve years. Last year Mr. Hardy made in this way 160,000 gallons of wine. He began life as a gold-digger. He commenced growing grapes for wine in 1853, and has been at it ever since. Another charming vineyard is that of Sir Samuel Davenport, to which Thomas Binney, when in Australia, was always ready to retreat. It is very interesting, this original vineyard of Mr. Hardy's. Since 1853 he has purchased several vineyards in various districts, the most important one being Tintara, about 25 miles to the South of Adelaide, where he has 150 acres under vines. It is in the town cellars that most of the blending is accomplished. A good deal of wine is bottled off at Bankside, but the main bulk of the generous fluid, to be poetical, is carted away in casks, on waggons which are as unromantic as the horses which draw them or the men who drive. There is little of the picturesque in the manufacture of Australian wine.

But as to the grounds, no words can describe their exuberance. Some of the pears Mr. Hardy exhibited at the London Exhibition weighed three pounds each, and were afterwards, I believe, eaten by Royalty. The Bankside property consists of a very deep chocolate soil, resting on a strong clay. Irrigation is easily practised over this small area. Water is raised from the bed of the Torrens River to the top of the bank, and, that being higher than the surrounding country, is easily distributed. It is curious what good a little water can accomplish. In one part the ground rises, and as water will not run uphill—at any rate, in Australia—the trees have to do without, and it is astonishing to note the difference between the trees and the fruit they bear, compared with the others, although but a few feet from each other. Everywhere around me were oranges ripening for the home market. 'An acre of oranges is a fortune, is it not?' I asked, with my head full of what I had read. 'Ah,' replied Mr. Hardy, with a smile, 'those books are written by men who have land to sell.' Then we came to the lemons. What a wonderful plant is the lemon tree! You may see the ripe fruit growing side-by-side with the blossom. It is productive all the year round, like—I will not say whose; let the reader fill up the blank—like Mr. ——'s great mind. As to the quinces, I never saw anything like them, and though I intimated that in

England we did not make much of them, Mr. Hardy assured me that in his opinion quince jam was the finest in the world. The citrons, however, were still finer than the quinces. We had also quite a show of olives; they grow in rows, and, like the almonds on the estate, they are made to do duty as fencing-posts. A vine in the open air over the house attracted my notice; it had spread over a surface of many yards, and was a good illustration of what may be done on Australian soil. Surely every Australian ought to grow his own grapes; and then as to making them into raisins and currants, nothing seems easier under such a sun. The grapes at Bankside are gathered and laid on boards to dry. Those for raisins for the table are laid on gravel—a custom Mr. Hardy borrowed from the Spaniards. It is not found necessary to turn them, the under grapes drying as well as the top ones, from the heat of the gravel floor. The turning of grapes into raisins is a more complicated process than merely growing them for the market. The bunches of ripe fruit are placed in oblong sieves and plunged for twenty seconds into a tank of boiling lye made from ashes, which are got from the vine prunings. The dipping takes the bloom off the fruit, but causes it to dry in one-third the time it would otherwise take. They are then spread evenly on wooden trays and exposed to the sun. When the grapes are about three-parts dried, they are removed to kilns, heated with hot-air pipes, and the drying is completed in from twelve to twenty-four hours, when they are taken out and rubbed partly free of most of the stalks. The next process is to run them through a winnowing machine which still further strips them of their stalk. They are then packed up in boxes by girls and pressed with a handy screw-press, six at a time. Currants are treated in a similar manner, minus the dipping. The raisins intended for the table, I may mention, are also not dipped, as that would spoil their appearance by removing the bloom. In the grounds a good many sultanas are also grown; quite equal to the fruit imported. Altogether, at Bankside, they turn out about twenty tons of dried fruit every year.

Australia, Mr. Hardy anticipates, will be able to equal the best wine districts in the world. A similar remark may apply to its almonds and raisins and currants. Adelaide rejoices in a trade which bids fair to become greater every year. As the Select Committee upon Vegetable Produce reported at the end of 1887: 'If the whole area of our colony now devoted to the growth of wheat were one vast vineyard, the yield would not be equal to the deficiency in the wine production of France through the devastation of the phylloxera.' Hence South Australia, to the disgust of Dr. Hannay, calculates much on her growing wine trade. Statistics furnished by Mr. Hayter, the Government Statist of Victoria, give evidence of the way in which wine in South Australia is superseding the consumption of spirits. This may account for the sobriety which seems to characterise South Australia as compared with the rest of the colonies. Altogether, Adelaide may claim to be the fairest city of Australia, and to contain the kindest and best-mannered people—so far as they may be judged by the passing stranger at their gates, and if I was in search of an ideal life I should say it would be that of one who sits under his own vine and figtree, as the South Australian grape-grower does.

While writing of wine, it may be as well to sum up here what I have to say on intemperance in Australia. No little excitement was produced in Adelaide when the writer was there by a telegraphic report of a speech by Dr. Hannay on his return from Australia, as to the amount of drinking in Adelaide, certainly the most sober of all the prosperous cities on the Australian Continent. As usual, the telegraphic report was wrong, and

Dr. Hannay assures me that what he did say was that he regretted to find that so many gentlemen in Adelaide looked to the increase of the Australian wine trade as a source of colonial revenue and colonial prosperity. As a devoted temperance reformer, it is clear Dr. Hannay could not have said less. It was an opinion which he was quite at liberty to utter, and with which no one could find fault. Had the telegraphic abridgment been correct, he would certainly have been to blame, as, undoubtedly, Adelaide is a sober city—that is, sober as compared with Sydney and Melbourne. In the older cities there are yet traces of the times when, as during the madness created by the discovery of alluvial gold, miners, who in England had been content with beer and porter, would drink twenty pounds' worth of champagne at a sitting, pouring it all into a pail, and asking every passer-by to have a drink; but that awful time of extravagance is past; however, the taint of it remains, and there is still a startling amount of drunkenness, especially among that part of the population who can least afford it—the wage-earning class, who, in Australia, if they are sober and industrious, have advantages in the way of investment which assuredly they lack at home. Workmen as a rule are paid high wages, and, when they receive a large amount at a time, as they often do, do not know what to do with it. In too many cases, in the interior more especially, they still adhere to the custom of knocking a cheque down, as they call it. The workman repairs to the nearest public-house, gives his cheque into the publican's hands, and then begins a drunken orgie in which everyone is asked to join, till the landlord tells him his money is all gone, gives him a bottle of rum, and then kicks him out of the house, often to perish by the road-side, thus once more illustrating the old remark, 'that the tender mercies of the wicked are very cruel.' One publican is said to have made £40,000 a year at one time in this way. The temperance reformers in Australia have, it is very evident, a wide field of usefulness before them. Many of the Australians spend enormous sums of money in drink. I travelled with an Australian, who seemed to me never what is vulgarly called the worse for liquor, yet whose weekly bill on board the steamer amounted to between four and five pounds, a sum of money which assuredly might have been better employed. In one respect Australia sets us a good example. It has taken to building temperance coffee hotels, or palaces, as they term them, on the grandest scale. As the meals are all served up without intoxicating drinks, these places must have a good effect, as the guest, however fond of drink he may be, is compelled for the time to be an abstainer. Adelaide unfortunately has no good temperance hotels worthy of the name.

It is a great question in Australia as to which is the finer city—Melbourne or Sydney—and the inhabitants of each are wonderfully jealous of each other. You offend a Melbourne man if you have anything to say in favour of Sydney, and at the latter city you hear little in favour of Melbourne. Both cities show too many public-houses, and both cities contain far too many drunkards; but in Sydney they are an especial nuisance, as every house has, as a rule, two rooms on each side the principal entrance which are used as bars, and which all day long, very much to the annoyance of the traveller, who is compelled to use them, are filled by a disreputable crowd, boozing from morning till night. It is the same as regards the theatre—the bar is as conspicuous, and quite as well filled, as the theatre itself. In many cases the bar is hired and carried on as a separate speculation, independently of the hotel proprietor. Two or three showy barmaids are engaged, a screen is put before the door to shield it from public gaze, and inside there is a license of which few people have an idea. The girls sell the drink, and they drink themselves.

As the evening advances the hilarity is of a somewhat boisterous character. Now and then a girl comes from behind the bar and waltzes round the room with some admirer—while she leers over his shoulder at another. The utmost freedom is permitted, and hundreds of idiots thus waste their time and spend their money, and injure their health, and learn how easy and how pleasant is the road to destruction. Fortunately, the bars are closed at eleven, and they are shut up on a Sunday, or they would be a great deal more mischievous than they really are; but the mischief they do is very great. In Australia the population is of an exceedingly shifting character; men are always on the move from one place to another, and of an evening, as they are strangers in the city and have no friends, and time hangs heavy on their hands, they have recourse to the nearest bar. It is there the sharper always takes his victim. In every case, and I heard of several, in which inexperienced travellers had been fleeced, I always found that the dupe had first been taken to the bar and treated to a drink. As I came back I fell in with a poor steerage passenger who had been done out of £20, a sum he could ill afford to lose, by a repetition of the confidence trick. He made the acquaintance of the sharper by means of the latter offering him a drink.

Hundreds and thousands of pounds have been lost in this way. There is no place so dangerous to a 'new chum,' as the emigrant to Australia is called, as the bar of a public-house. Alas! in Sydney these pitfalls are on every side; I think that there is only one hotel in the town without its bar.

It was the old custom to sell lots of land by auction at which a good deal of wine was drunk, under the excitement produced by which many a purchaser bought his whistle at a dearer price. 'If such lunches cost £40,' writes one of the oldest of the Melbourne colonists, Mr. Westgarth, 'which was given to me as a moderate average, who suffered? argued their justifiers; the exhilaration they produced gave £400 more to the net proceeds.' The brisk liquor appreciably blew up the prices, as the same lots, cut up and rearranged, would come again and yet again under the hammer; and no doubt many a poor speculator burnt his fingers in that way, especially when we remember how at one time there came such a wonderful depreciation of property in what its admirers still love to term 'Marvellous Melbourne.' It may be that there is less drinking now, and that people go to business and to sales with less muddled brains. But no one can walk in the shipping quarter of Melbourne on a Saturday afternoon, or stop at a Sydney hotel for a day or two, without feeling that in either town there is vast room for improvement in the matter of drink. In both places there is a fearful amount of gambling and betting and wild speculation, and undoubtedly a good deal of that goes on under the influence of the drink. Many of the suicides which, as I told the people of Adelaide, were such a matter of wonderment to me, are to be attributed to drink, or the depression caused by it when the excitement is over, and the poor shattered drinker is, indeed, a cup too low and quite unable in his dazed condition to face the stern realities of life. Travelling one day from Brisbane to Sydney, the writer met a gentleman, of whom he asked if Mr. Blank was known to him.

'Yes, well,' was the reply.

'I am going to see him.'

'Why,' said the gentleman, 'he committed suicide only a little while ago; and the Western Australian papers are full of the details.'

There was no need to say any more. The poor fellow had gone out as an emigrant. At home he had been in the habit of drinking to excess, and in Australia the loneliness and difficulty of his life was too much for him; he drank to excess, and then took away with his own rash hand his blighted life. In Australia the number of such blighted lives through drink is far too plentiful.

CHAPTER XII.

AN AUSTRALIAN MILLIONAIRE.

Mr. James Tyson.

As I was seated in the dining-saloon of the *Orizaba*, an Australian, pointing to a particular table, remarked to me that there were three millionaires dining there. I am no company for such. They are out of my sphere. However, one of them kindly invited me to dine with him in Melbourne. I would like to have accepted the invitation. Alas! I was engaged to dine elsewhere. One would like to dine with a millionaire. Tom Hood evidently did, or he would not have told how

> 'The company ate and drank from gold,
>   They revelled, they sang, and were merry;
> And one of the gold sticks rose from his chair,
> And toasted the "Lass with the golden hair,"
>   In a bumper of golden sherry.'

According to popular report, the great millionaires

of Australia are Mr. James Tyson, six millions; Sir William Clarke, three; and Mr. George Lawson, one and a half.

James Tyson, the well-known Australian millionaire, was born near Sydney in 1823. His father was the scion of a good old Cumberland family, but having offended his parents by marriage against their wishes, he found things so unpleasant at home that he enlisted in the army. His discharge was purchased in 1818, when he emigrated from England in the service of Mr. Commissioner Bigge, who was sent out to investigate the charges against Governor Macquarie. In time, he commenced his career as a farmer, and died. His son, after assisting his mother on her farm, entered the service of a firm of agriculturists, on a salary of £30 a year. Many were his ups and downs. At one time he had to go to a station for a draft of cattle, which were to be placed under the care of himself and brother. James Tyson, to prepare himself for his journey, cooked as many rations as he could carry on his horse, and of money he had just one shilling, which was demanded of him by the ferryman for taking him with his horse over the Murrumbidgee. Declining to part with his shilling, he swam over the river, if not at the risk of his life, greatly to the detriment of his rations. Again, we find him in another part of the colony, where, while his brother kept a dairy, James went jobbing and cattle-driving, until a few of his cattle were fat, and fit for market. He afterwards, with the neighbouring stock-owners, sold a lot at Sydney. He and his brother, in time, obtained possession of a run near the junction of the Lachland and Murrumbidgee rivers. In 1851, when the gold discoveries were made, James Tyson commenced cattle-driving to Sandhurst, where he opened up a large business as a butcher, wholesale and retail, and where he made a good deal of money. After carrying on business successfully till 1855, he made some purchases of stations, and next extended his operations to Queensland. He afterwards acquired several immense stations on the Warrego, where, as in Victoria and New South Wales, he now holds large areas of freehold land. His mother is naturally very proud of her distinguished son. When the Duke of Edinburgh was in the colony he was taken to see the old lady. 'There,' said the old woman, as the Prince bade her good-bye, 'you can tell your mother you have shaken hands with Jem Tyson's mother,' and no doubt the message was faithfully reported.

Mr. Tyson is a broad-shouldered, robust man, standing 6 feet $3\frac{1}{2}$ inches high. He has never had a day's illness in his life; has lived much in the open air, and prefers it ; is a keen sportsman, and a good shot. Nevertheless, he is a good deal of a vegetarian. On one occasion, it is said, according to the custom of the country, in the course of his travels he rode up to a station for a night's lodging. 'Oh, is that you?' said the woman of the house. 'You can go and hobble yourself,' throwing him the leathern straps by means of which the Australian colonists hobble their horses for the night. The millionaire is reported often to indulge in an economical supper of boiled grass, and hence the woman's allusion. A stricter teetotaler there is not in Australia. Mr. Tyson has never indulged in a glass of wine or spirits in his life, nor has he ever smoked an ounce of tobacco. It is to be questioned whether he would have had such a successful career as he has marked out for himself, had he indulged in the drinking customs which were the disgrace of all Australia at one time. He owes his good fortune almost entirely to his energy, his untiring industry, and his great self-denial. He is a true friend and a staunch protector of the aborigines on his various stations, who are all much attached to him, and render willing service. He is of a very retiring disposition, and has always refused to allow parliamentary or any other public honours to be thrust upon him. He is a bachelor, and mingles but little in society—is, however, very fond of children, and has always been a liberal supporter of all local schools and other popular institutions, though generally averse to having his name paraded before the public. The exact amount of his wealth is not known, but he is supposed to have amassed from four to six millions, and, on one occasion, he offered the Government of Queensland the loan of half a million towards the construction of a trans-continental railway. Those who know him best, say of him as Disraeli said of Gladstone, 'He has not one redeeming vice.' It is to his credit that his temper is so even that, under the most trying circumstances, no profane word has ever been heard to escape from his lips. On one occasion, riding late at night to one of his many stations, he was refused admission by the keeper, to whom he told his name in vain, as the man did not believe him. He slept out that night, and, when he returned in the morning, rewarded the man handsomely for his obedience to orders. Of course Mr. Tyson is not very popular. He is too wealthy to be that. Impecunious people always make a dead set at a millionaire, and are very wrath if he does not see his way to set them on their legs again, or, at any rate, to give them a start in life. 'The simplicity and frugality of his habits,' observes Mr. Henniker-Heaton, M.P., from whom I borrow most of the particulars of this sketch, 'should disarm the envy of those who might be disposed to covet his great riches.' Alas! the reverse is the case. I found few who had a good word to say of the richest man in any of the Australian colonies, and all sorts of wild stories are told of him—even as to his exploits when in a state of alleged drunkenness. Mr. Tyson has, at any rate, one fault, and that is he is a very great hater of women; he even dislikes, I was told, to employ married men. 'He sees no good in having a man who is under the influence of a woman.' Clearly he holds that no man can serve two masters. Poor fellow! I asked:

'What is to become of all his wealth?'

'It will help to make work for the lawyers,' was the somewhat cynical reply.

We admire Mr. Tyson for his abstinence, and for his energy, his industry, and economy. In this respect he sets the Australians a good example, but he is not a model to be followed in every respect. The best of us, it is to be feared, are poor creatures after all.

CHAPTER XIII.

AUSTRALIAN FACTS AND FIGURES.

Increase of the Colonies—Further Emigration Required—New South Wales and Free-trade—The Australian Type.

STATISTICS are not pleasant reading. They are so easily twisted to serve the writer's purpose rather than to develop the real truth of the case, but to please certain readers who are always wanting to know, I give the Australasian statistics for 1888 laid before the New South Wales Parliament, which show another year of steady progress on the part of these colonies. The total population of Australasia on December 31 last is estimated at 3,672,803, Victoria standing highest with 1,090,869; New South Wales, 1,085,740; New Zealand, 607,380; South Australia, 313,065; Queensland, 387,463; Tasmania, 146,149; Western Australia, 42,137. The total increase for the year was 126,077, the Queensland ratio of increase being 5·59; Victoria, 5·28; New South Wales, 4·10; Tasmania, 2·57 ; New Zealand, ·66 ; South Australia, ·21 ; while Western Australia showed a decrease of 351 persons, or ·82 per cent. There was a total of 26,584 marriages, 122,982 births, and 48,400 deaths last year ; the average birth-rate per 1,000 being 34·05, and death-rate 13·40. The number of immigrants and emigrants during the year was respectively 24,889 and 188,230, the excess of emigrants being 65,599. The Victorian net gain by immigration was 41,803 ; that of New South Wales, 21,545 ; Queensland, 11,805 ; whilst in South Australia there were 113 less immigrants than emigrants, Western Australia being on the same side of the balance to the extent of 1,196, and New Zealand to the extent of 9,175. Of sheep the Australian Colonies possess 96,487,811. Of these New South Wales has 48·20 per cent. ; Victoria, 11·20 ; Queensland, 13·93 ; South Australia, 7·41. Horned cattle, total 9,248,949, New South Wales possessing 17·54 per cent. ; Victoria, 14·19 ; Queensland, 50·32 ; South Australia, 4·65. Horses amount to 1,136,683, New South Wales having 21·88 per cent. ; Victoria, 21·31 ; Queensland, 6·07 ; South Australia, 14·95. The imports for the colonies in 1888 were : New South Wales, £20,885,557 ; Victoria, £23,972,134 ; South Australia, £5,413,638 ; Queensland, £6,544,324. Exports : New South Wales, £20,859,715 ; Victoria,

£13,853,763; South Australia, £6,984,098; Queensland, £5,226,929. Total imports and exports for the whole of the colonies, £121,859,908, or £33 15s. 2d. per head. New South Wales, Victoria, South Australia, and Western Australia exceeded this average, whilst the other colonies were considerably below it. The total tonnage entered and cleared at Australian ports amounted to 14,689,766 tons, of which New South Wales represented 4,765,419 tons; Victoria, 4,307,883 tons; South Australia, 1,973,651 tons.

In answer to the question why Australia does not attract a far larger European emigration, the reply is, the mistaken policy of the Australian Parliament. The working man in Australia is opposed to it, and M.P.'s truckle to his wishes. An Australian M.P. is paid, and he naturally wishes to retain his pay, and hence he bows to the majority, whether right or wrong. If English emigrants went to Australia, as they do to Canada or America, the Australian colonies would flourish, labour would be cheap, agriculture would prosper, and the railways would be filled with passengers whose payments would enable them to yield good dividends. Mr. Macfie, a gentleman who resided ten years in Australia, and who is a master of Australian statistics, in a paper read before the Royal Colonial Society last year, contended that the most urgently needed aid to Australian development is selecting British and European population suitable for settlement on the land, and for raising productions for which there is a large demand in the colonies, the United Kingdom, and in foreign countries. Under the present system of government, this seems to be quite out of the question. He describes, for instance, the operatives of Victoria as organized into a compact phalanx under leaders who have succeeded by dogged persistence in imbuing the colony with the notion that they constitute the party which controls the voting power at elections. 'So widely,' says Mr. Macfie, 'is this assumption believed, that candidates for the Legislative Assembly, to whom a Parliamentary salary or political influence is a consideration, defer with real or affected humility to the wishes of the Trades Hall Council of Melbourne. The inevitable outcome of this state of political subjection on the part of members of the House, and in many cases of the Government also, is the injustice of class legislation. On the unjustifiable plea that the tendency of emigration is to reduce the rate of wages in the colony, the working-classes make no secret of their determination that the Government shall be prohibited from taking steps to encourage immigration of any kind, or even to diffuse information systematically, by pamphlets and lectures throughout Europe, in localities where thousands are thirsting to learn about Australia, and who would gladly proceed thither at their own cost, and engage in profitable branches of land culture.' It is really discouraging to find that while the Argentine Confederation receives an addition to its population on an average of 7,000 a week, and the United States 10,000, Australia, with its splendid climate and other advantages, only attracts a little over 1,000 persons, old and young, male and female, per week. This state of things is mischievous in many ways. It is not pleasant to find that, as Mr. Herbert Tritton pointed out, the Australasian Government debts increase in a very much larger ratio than the population. On this head Mr. Macfie makes a rather alarming statement. 'I have,' he said, 'recently been informed that a large investor in Australasian securities, deeply impressed with the necessity of investigating this subject for himself, proceeded to Australasia for the purpose of doing so. He returned to England convinced that in most of the self-governing colonies the working classes were barring the door against any effort whatsoever being made to promote immigration, extend widely agricultural settlement, and thus develop export wealth to Europe and America. He arrived at the conclusion that there was a tendency in the Local Governments and Parliaments to pander to the prejudices of those who indiscriminately discourage the introduction of even desirable immigrants. The belief was forced upon him that it is no sufficient answer to the fears of the bondholders to say that the money lent by them goes into reproductive works, such as railways. He saw railways constructed to serve an extremely sparse population in country districts, instead of a population twenty times the size, which would have rendered the line proportionately remunerative, had as much care been taken to attract people from Europe as to obtain British capital to build new lines for the limited number of settlers established in the districts through which they pass. The result of that visitor's observation was that he sold out—I think, with unwarrantable haste—his interest in Australasian stocks on his return home. Whether his views are correct or erroneous is not the question.'

The one colony that seems to flourish most is New South Wales, under a system of Free Trade, which, however, I fear is losing its popularity every day. 'Compared with the other colonies,' said Sir Henry Parkes, when I was there—' the only statesman in the colonies,' observed a gentleman to me one day—the popular Premier of New South Wales, ' New South Wales was the oldest, the richest and the most powerful. Ten or twelve years ago Victoria was far in advance of this colony—a quarter of a million of population in advance of us; but now we were in advance of her, and intended to keep in advance of her. In no other country in the world,' said Sir Henry, ' had any-one a chance of making a fortune as he had in New South Wales, and yet how melancholy is the spectacle, only peopled, as it were, on the fringe, with cities congested, while the land remained untilled; with all Europe waiting to buy if the colonies would but attract people to settle on its vacant lands and till its soil.'

Naturally you ask whether there is arising a distinct type of Australian. I think there is. The young Australian is tall, dark, has high cheek-bones and prominent teeth. Dr. MacLaurin, who lived a long time in Australia, and who is able to form a better opinion on the subject, in a paper read before the British Association, says in New South Wales and in Tasmania three generations have been exposed to the new conditions, and the greatgrandchildren of the first settlers cannot be distinguished from Englishmen, Scotchmen, or Irishmen, by anything in 'configuration and type.' There is no essentially *Australian* type of man. It is true that we find a certain 'sallowness in complexion' among the inhabitants of the colonies, but this may be observed also among those who have been only a few years resident there. It is due, Dr. MacLaurin thinks, much more to the effects of the sun's rays on the skin than to any *anæmia* arising from climate. The alleged 'lankiness' of the Australians is also very much a myth. Dr. MacLaurin can find no trace of it, after twenty years of experience in connection with assurance society examinations. He thinks, if it exists at all, it is only during the period of youth, when growth goes on more rapidly and under healthier conditions than in Europe. 'The fact is, the Australian youth are, as a whole, better fed, better clad, and better lodged than the inhabitants of Europe. They are not so much exposed to the inclemencies of the weather, and they are not obliged to work too hard or too early.' Hence the tendency to a 'tall, active, and athletic figure.' With regard to muscular vigour, the Australian has proved himself well able to hold his own in the struggle for existence. If we think only of the great love of out-door life, of athletic sports, of racing, rowing, cricketing, and the like, manifested by all native Australians, we shall come to the conclusion that they certainly are not deficient in muscular force. Dr. MacLaurin thinks the native Australian has no need to fear comparison with the youth of the mother land. The professors in the universities and colleges assure us that Australians are quite as bright and capable as the youth in British schools of learning; and Australian young men who study in Europe are always able to take a high position in intellectual competitions. Some of them, indeed, have recently taken the very highest places. When this subject is studied from the standpoint of longevity and fertility, we find the same excellent results. It is true that the deaths among persons over sixty-five years of age are more numerous here than in England, but every decade the standard of age is increasing, and when we take the general death-rate, we find that New South Wales is decidedly healthy as compared with any part of Great Britain and Ireland. In like manner the native Australian is as able as anyone to resist disease, which is only another way of saying that his physique is thoroughly healthy and capable of great endurance.

People at home have curious ideas as to Australian distances. I was asked to see a woman employed in some charitable institution near Sydney. When I got to Sydney, on asking for that particular locality, I was told it was seventy-two miles off.

One sees a great many people who enjoy life in Australia who could not live at home. That is one great charm of a country which, as has been well remarked, would get on very well if the inhabitants would grumble less at the climate and dam the rivers more.

The whites and the blacks do not seem yet to have hit on a *modus vivendi*. It is true the savant does not do as he did in the old times, coolly shoot a black when he wanted to add a skull to his collection. But while I was in Queensland a couple of whites did fire on a black, and a black did kill a white. Under the new constitution to be granted to Western Australia, the aborigines are to be placed under the care of a Commissioner, independent of the Parliament, and responsible only to the Governor. £5,000 a year is to be devoted to the purpose, but it is not clear how a body without police organization can watch and protect the inhabitants of a thousand square miles. I quote a case which occurred to show how matters are at present. In March last the blacks near Kimberley speared the horses of a man named Howard. Whether Howard had given them just cause I am unable to say. Howard himself evidently thought they were the aggressors, as he, with the assistance of a constable, followed them, and shot some three or four. The affair came to the ears of justice, and Howard and the constable were put on their trial for murder. They were acquitted, of course, owing to the absence of direct proof that any lives were actually taken, and owing to the doubts that existed as to whether they simply fired at the blacks on coming up to them, or resorted to arms in self-defence.

The forests want looking after. In New South Wales, Victoria, New Zealand, and South Australia, the Governments are growing alive to the fact that the forests cannot last for ever. In many districts the traveller passes through hundreds of miles of ring-barked country, very desolate to look upon. It is pleasant to note that in some quarters steps have been taken to find a remedy. Especially is this the case in South Australia. Last year as many as 40,000 trees were sent out from the State nursery for planting.

The land question gives a good deal of trouble. It has, in New South Wales, much to answer for, as the great want of the farmer is water, and he will not improve his property by sinking Artesian wells, at a cost of £1,000 each, unless he has a better title. On the other hand, it is held that Victorian prosperity is chiefly due to its liberal land laws. In New South

Wales the farmer is given 2,500 acres with no cultivation conditions. He can hold it as he gets it till his time is up, and transfer it to the squatter, and then go and re-select as long and as often as he likes, with this result, that there is no real settlement in the land—no progress, and no employment for the agricultural labourer.

CHAPTER XIV.

COMING HOME.

The Sea—Colombo—Arabi—Ceylon Tea—Stoppage in the Canal—Tilbury Docks—The Future of Australia—Australia as a Field for Emigration.

ONCE more I am afloat. I bid good-bye to a friend who was six months coming out, and lived on salt beef and pork all the while. In this respect we have changed for the better. But the sea, is it ever to be depended on?

According to the Duc de Joinville, when Saint Louis, King of France, was on his return journey from the Holy Land, whither he had been to fight the Saracen, off Cyprus the ship ran aground, and all were in deadly peril. But the King refused to get into another ship, preferring, he tells us, 'to entrust to God's keeping my own life and the lives of my wife and children, rather than ensure so much hurt to such a large number of persons as are on board.' Few of us have attained to such saintship, and, as a matter of fact, as regards most of us, our trust in supernatural interposition is that of the old woman of whom Mr. Gough used to tell us who, when asked how she felt when the horse ran away, replied that she trusted in Providence till the reins broke, and then she gave up. Alas, in a stormy sea, in a moment of peril from collision, or in case of a ship foundering, in the mad struggle for life it seems as if, in spite of all science has yet achieved, as if there were no power, human or divine, to ward off that cruel death, which in that hour of agony seems to ride the whirlwind and direct the storm ; and day by day, and now more than ever, we hear of tragedies at sea which make the cheek of the landsman, even if he has no loved ones to lament, turn pale, and his heart to sicken. It is true ships carry boats, but they are smashed in launching, or they are launched too late, or they are upset ; or if not, they carry no provisions, or are found deficient in oars, and the chances are if help comes in the shape of a friendly ship that has seen the signal from afar, only a few survive to tell the sad tale of cold and wet and hunger and thirst, under the fearful pressure of which their shipmates have succumbed. In the House of Commons, the other day, an M.P. suggested that an Act of Parliament should be passed compelling every ship to carry as many boats as would accommodate all the crew and passengers—an utter impossibility. Clearly it is not in that direction that we are to look for help. It consoles one to reflect, however, that the commanders and officers of our Australian steamers rarely run their ships into danger, and manage when in it to get out again.

It is in the dark watches of the night that a passenger feels most timid. A lady assured me, the other day, whenever it was rough she lay awake all night expecting the ship to go to the bottom. I endeavoured to give her what comfort I could ; but night in the tropics is slightly awful. The sun drops down into the waters in such a glare of angry red. The clouds that come, or rather fly, with the early dawn seem so dark and threatening, and then the ocean has ever a melancholy wail. These almost leave me sometimes absolutely awestruck. It is not in this case true that familiarity breeds contempt.

At length I lay down my pen so far as the great country of Australia is concerned. I have skirted its coast for many a hundred miles. I have tarried in its cities, have seen some of its best men and women, and have gone up into the interior, where population is scarce and life is of the simplest and roughest. I came back by the dear old *Liguria* from Sydney to Melbourne, was carried by the *Austral* to Adelaide, and then left Adelaide by the *Iberia*, 'the best ship of the line,' said an old Australian to me, with a captain, whose name is Shannon, as fond of a good game of chess as myself, and who did much to make me and all his passengers comfortable. The *Iberia* is not such a grand ship as the *Orizaba*, and its smoking-room was uncomfortably small, but we managed to enjoy ourselves after we had left Cape Leeuwin, always washed by a stormy sea, and found ourselves once more on the Indian Ocean, calm all the way as a mill-pond, but hot as a furnace in full blast. What a relief it was to see Adam's Peak, and green Ceylon, and Colombo; to exchange my warm clothing for the white suit of clothing the Cingalese tailor makes up for you while the ship is coaling, and to go on shore and take a ride along the parks and flower-gardens and cocoanut-groves of the gem of the Indian Ocean, as Colombo is fitly called! On my return I was exceptionally fortunate. Mr. John Fergusson, of the *Colombo Observer*, had seen my name in the list of passengers, and, with a kindness for which I cannot be too grateful, had sent a native messenger on board to take me on shore—a brown, slightly-dressed young gentleman, whose broken

English helped at any rate to while away the time, and to make me forget the awful heat. Mr. Fergusson, after a warm reception—all the more agreeable as up to that time I had not even known his name—being an editor and too busy to give me much of his time, handed me over to the care of his pastor, the Rev. Mr. Durbin, a Baptist minister, whose chapel is one of the most attractive places of worship in the town, and whose congregation, I found, was in a very flourishing condition. In company with this gentleman, I inspected the oldest ecclesiastical building at Colombo, the old Dutch church, built much after the fashion that prevails in Holland to this day. Then we did the Law Courts, a pile of white buildings, forming a perfect square, crowded all day long with natives, who are never so happy as when at law with each other. The courts were lofty and airy, and the crowd of half-dressed witnesses and criminals were kept at a respectful distance. The proceedings were somewhat slow, as the evidence had to be translated into English for the benefit of the presiding genius. Native police guarded both the exterior and interior, and in the library I was introduced to several native barristers—very fine, manly-looking men—whose manners and appearance were of the most unexceptionable character. In company with Mrs. Fergusson, I visited the far-famed Arabi Pasha, in his picturesque place of exile—a well-made Egyptian, in the dress of his country, who received us politely, but the conversation we carried on was not of very thrilling character. The gentleman is shy of interviewers. A correspondent one day had called on him, and to his disgust the whole conversation was related in a London newspaper. Consequently, now, Arabi says little, though, perhaps, he thinks the more. One of our party had taken Mr. Caine, when in Colombo, to call, but the English M.P. failed to get much out of the wily Egyptian, though he tried him in every possible way. Nor was Arabi much more communicative to myself. He seemed to me weary of his exile. Indeed, he told me he would prefer London to Colombo. 'He ought not to dislike the English,' said a resident in Suez to me. 'He would have been murdered had he stopped there. He has no friends in Egypt; the Egyptians always kick a man when he is down.' I returned to the *Iberia* in a catamaran, and with a box of the finest Ceylon tea, kindly given me by Mr. Fergusson, and which, for the benefit of my home readers, I may mention may be procured of Messrs. Swan, Laurence Pountney Lane, London, dealers in Ceylon tea exclusively.

We had the usual fine, hot weather up the Red Sea. I had a disagreeable attack of what is called prickly heat—the only consolation, and it was a real one, being that the weather-wise assured me that if I had not had it, I should have had something worse. We did not call at Aden, nor were we sorry for that, as most of us had got rather tired of the long travel and exhausting heat. Already we had had three deaths on board, and were eager to be safe at home. One morning the captain pointed to our left, and told me that on one of the islands far away in that direction the woman is master, and the man has to take the back-seat. It would have been interesting if we could have gone there and seen how they got on, but mail steamers are bound to keep on their proper course. He who would study the islands and waste places of the Indian Ocean must have a yacht to himself—and there is a good deal to be learned, which can be got at in no other way. In due time we were in the Canal—alas! there to remain all night at anchor, with the lights of old Suez in the distance, which we were afraid to visit, as we might be off at any moment. The Egyptians, with their donkeys on the beach, all night long screamed to us to come on shore and have a ride. At length, the *Katie*, of West Hartlepool, which had grounded and stopped our passage, was got off, and we made our way to Port Said, which did not prove more attractive on a second visit than it did on the first. Of course I went on shore to look at the veiled women and bearded men, to be attacked by the sellers of cigars and rubbish of all kinds, and to get very tired of the place, which, however, must do a good deal of business in the course of the year.

Cooler weather comes to us as we sail through the Straits of Messina, and pass snow-capped Etna afar off. We stop at Naples to set down the mails and take up passengers. We are full to suffocation. My cabin, too small for myself to live in in comfort, has to submit to intrusion : but old gentlemen who have been spending the winter abroad with their wives and families have to be accommodated.

At Gibraltar we stop to take up a few more passengers, and to buy Spanish fans and Moorish trifles. It really does strike one how, as you approach the Rock from the Mediterranean, it resembles a huge lion, with its back on Africa, and its face looking towards Spain. In the Bay of Biscay there is what the meteorologists call a slight depression, which means a little rolling; all that we have had to encounter since we left Cape Leeuwin. The rolling, more or less, accompanies us to Plymouth, where we arrive at night. The knowing ones get out, and proceed to London by train, as they say we shall catch it in the Channel. As usual, the knowing ones are wrong. Who but a fool will talk with certainty about horses, wine, women, or weather? It is fine, beautifully fine, till we get to Deal, when down come the heavens in waterfalls of rain. It rains all night as we lie at anchor there, waiting for the daylight to take us to Tilbury Docks, to be examined by Custom House officers in the huge shed where all the luggage is landed, and the Queen's taxes paid. This is a place where a passenger need have sharp eyes. I found, after a good deal of trouble, a beautiful fur rug, which happened to be mine, in a place where it had no right to be. It is hard on the passenger, that Custom House shed, and by the time the poor fellow is shot out at Fenchurch Street, where he has to seek his scattered luggage at the hazard of his life, it is not much to be wondered at if he resolves never to take an Australian trip again.

I must own, however, that no such feeling entered into my head. The difficulties which at one time beset the traveller are unknown. He is at home among friends. It is said the last of the Australian Bush Rangers now keeps an hotel in San Francisco, so there is little to fear. My experiences in Australia remain in my memory, and will long remain, as among the brightest and pleasantest of a life mercifully varied and protracted more than that of many. I have seen a sunny land, rich in all that men hold dear, where our brethren have planted another Britain—minus the State Church, in which few of us believe, and the aristocratic element, which all the world over has had its day. Democracy has grown to be the ruler of the world, and in Australia the experiment, so far as it has been tried, is a success. Material wealth abounds, and statesmen have provided that ignorance shall be banished the new community; while the religious of all denominations have shown how churches are to be built and preachers provided, and Christ's kingdom advanced better without a State Church than with it. In many parts, especially in Adelaide, I was the recipient of a graceful and lavish hospitality impossible to conceive of at home. There, also, I found a civilization as refined, an energy it may be greater, a hope—as regards this world, at any rate—more secure. If we have to mourn over a Paradise Lost, in Australia we realize a Paradise Regained. Of the Australian, I may emphatically say that his lines are cast in pleasant places, and that he has a goodly heritage. Whether he will long remain a colonist I more than doubt. The colonies, I hold, are prepared for separation; but, when it does come, it will be not from choice, but necessity. So long as no practical difficulties arise, matters will remain as they are.

Is Australia a fitting field for emigration? Will it provide our starving East-enders with good living and good homes? And can the young man of the middle-class find there the opening for his energies denied him here? The last question I am rather inclined to answer in the affirmative—if he has his head on his shoulders—if he does not rate his own services too highly—if he does not refuse the first opportunity that comes in his way. Friends he will find in the colony ready to lend him a helping hand, and in most of the towns there is a branch of the Christian Young Men's Association, the secretary of which is generally in a position to give him suitable advice. It is a fact that people do well as a rule, and that, thanks to the climate, the tender-chested and delicate have a better prospect of healthy life than in our damp and fog-crowned island. In a land flooded with glorious sunshine, poverty loses some of its bitterness, for in Australia the blue sky and the bright sun are the heritage of all. As to our very poor—whom we gladly ship off—as a rule I question whether they would be much benefited by being shot out into the poor quarters of the great Australian towns and cities. They are too feeble to stand alone. There is no help for them as long as they breed as awfully as they do at the East End. Charity seeks to supply their needs in vain, and as to State interference, the less we have of that the better. The strong, self-reliant, clear-headed working-man—the man who can get on at home—will get on out there ; as will also the capitalist who knows how to invest his money. A man who is in a good position at home, however, would be a fool to throw it up for the sake of a chance in the land of the Golden Fleece.

THE END.

GREEN'S BLACKWALL LINE

AND

Devitt & Moore's Australian Line.

CARLISLE CASTLE.
COLLINGWOOD.
DERWENT.
HARBINGER.
HESPERUS.
ILLAWARRA.

MACQUARIE.
MERMERUS.
RODNEY.
SOBRAON.
TAMAR.
Etc., Etc.

THESE splendid vessels sail regularly to and from Australia, and offer unequalled advantages to passengers travelling for health or pleasure. Each vessel carries a surgeon.

F. GREEN & CO.,

13, FENCHURCH AVENUE,

LONDON, E.C.

www.ingramcontent.com/pod-product-compliance
Lightning Source LLC
Chambersburg PA
CBHW020805230426
43666CB00007B/861